Spiritual Awakening

My way to life

Ragnar Viktor Karlsson

This book is about you and your way to life.

It becomes true only when you've experienced it.

Contents

Contents

The Early Years

In the spring of 1970, my parents rented an apartment in a small wooden house at Tjarnargata 3 in Reykjavík with my grandparents. We didn't live there for long, and I don't remember this home at all. After we moved out in 1972, the house burned to the ground, and the site was turned into a parking lot.

On the morning of April 22, 1970, my grandfather ran out to the fire station at Tjarnargata 10 to get an ambulance for my mother because I was about to be born. Later that day, I was born at a birthing center in Reykjavík.

My earliest memories are from Ásvallagata 4 in Reykjavík, where my parents rented a basement apartment. My grandparents had moved to a different apartment in Reykjavík.

My parents both worked, and during the day I stayed with a woman named Ida in Steinahlíð. I enjoyed my time with Ida. She was strict, but deep down she was kind and loving and took good care of the children who stayed with her. We became close friends. I usually arrived first, so we often had fun together in the morning before the other children arrived. She lived in a small room in the loft in Steinahlíð. The stairs leading up to the room were almost vertical. If I got sick in the middle of the day, she would take me to her room. She let me sleep there until my mother came to pick me up in the afternoon.

Ragnar Viktor Karlsson

In the spring of 1976, I stopped going to Steinahlíð. I was six years old, and my time there was over. I still remember my last day, as the entire day I stayed close to Ida and repeated, "This is my last day. My dad will come get me later."

Ida smiled and patted me on the head. "It'll be OK. You can always come and visit. You're always welcome, my friend."

My father picked me up, and as we gathered all my things, I ran to Ida and put my arms around her. Tears ran down my cheeks as I said goodbye. I looked out the back window of the car as we drove out of the driveway. An adventure that had lasted for several years was over.

I visited Ida several times after that, and she always welcomed me. We always had a fun time together.

The time I spent with my great-grandfather and great-grandmother, who lived at Hófgerði 12 in Kópavogur, was also quite memorable. I used to visit them with my mother on the weekends. It was a great adventure to go to Hófgerdi 12. My great-grandfather had a small sheep shed on the property, and the sheep grazed in a large garden by the house. My great-grandfather was always teaching and mentoring me, and we spent many hours together in the sheep shed and his workshop. We often went for long walks around the neighborhood and looked at the Kópavogur church that stood on the hill above.

Sometimes I got to stay the night at Hófgerði. I remember when it got dark, I would sit for hours at the table by the kitchen sink and watch the lighthouse in Öskjuhlíð. First, the green light appeared and then went out. After a long time, the white light appeared and then went out, and then the green light appeared again. This repeated again and again, and I watched this interplay between light and darkness with fascination.

Back on Ásvallagata, there was a small garden in front of the house we lived in where I could play in the grass. As I was the only child in my family and in the entire house, I quickly learned to play alone, and I often talked to myself while I was playing.

I still remember my first spiritual experience at home on Ásvallagata. I was just beginning to speak when my mother started teaching me how to pray. She told me about Jesus Christ and God. One evening, when I was lying in bed and ready to sleep and the only light in the room was the lamp on my bedside table, my mother came to me and said, "Now I will teach you the Lord's prayer."

I sat up in bed and said, "Lord's prayer, what's that?"

"Lie down now. We ask God and Jesus to protect us and watch over us and care for us while we sleep."

I listened to my mother and began to think.

"Now, fold your hands and close your eyes." She began, "Our Father who art in heaven . . ." and I repeated, "Our Father who art in heaven . . ." We went through the entire Lord's prayer like that.

Ragnar Viktor Karlsson

When we had said "amen," my mother said to me, "Now God and Jesus will watch over you tonight. Good night and sleep well." She turned off the lamp on the nightstand and left the room.

I lay in bed and looked around the room. After each time we said the Lord's prayer, I felt a calm come over me and fill the room. I feared nothing, neither the darkness nor the solitude. I saw Jesus standing beside God in heaven. They were on a white cloud, and God was an old man with white hair and a beard who had a long stick in his hand. I sensed that they were watching and looking out for me. I drifted to sleep in my little bed. This was my first spiritual experience.

In 1976, my mother's brothers and my great-grandfather bought the farm Sólbakki in Þykkvabær. That spring, I sensed that something was off in our home. The atmosphere between my parents was strange. Then, one spring day, my mother was busy packing things into boxes and bags. My belongings went into boxes along with her things. When I asked her where we were going, she replied, "We're moving to the countryside in Þykkvabær to the east of here."

I found the idea very exciting. "Won't we come back here?" I wondered.

"No, we're moving away from here," she replied.

My father lay on the couch in the living room reading a book. I went up to him and said, "Won't you pack your stuff?"

4

He looked up from the book and at me. "I'll come later, buddy."

I felt that something was out of the ordinary. I knew in my heart that he would not be coming later and that their relationship was over.

When all our stuff was in the moving van, my mother said, "Well, let's go now."

I ran to my father, who was still lying in the living room, and put my arms around him to say goodbye. "Bye, Dad," I said, holding him tight.

"Have a good time at the farm," he replied.

Sitting in the back seat of the car, I looked out the window at the house we had lived in for several years. Saying goodbye to my father and our home was strange and difficult. We drove off, and I started asking my mother about the countryside and what would happen. The hour and a half it took to drive east to Þykkvabær seemed like an eternity to me because I had never sat in a car for so long before. As we approached the village, I saw the tiny houses slowly appear out of the ground. As we got closer, the houses grew bigger, and the church tower was most prominent. Eventually, we drove into the village.

The first thing I saw was a store we drove by, and shortly, we drove into the driveway in Sólbakki, which was now my new home. When we got to the house, I heard a dog barking loudly by the car. "What's that?" I asked my mother in alarm.

"This is Lucky. He came with the house, and he'll be our dog." My mother opened the car door, and the barking got even louder. I didn't like it and didn't budge from the back seat. Lucky had started sniffing my mother and wagged his tail eagerly. "Come on out, buddy, he's happy to see us," my mother said, holding out her hand. I cautiously got out of the car and stood still with both hands close to my chest while the dog sniffed me all over. He looked happy and wagged his tail. Lucky was an all-white Scottish-Icelandic sheepdog with a pink nose. Slowly, I lowered my hands and let him sniff them. Finally, I started petting him, and by then the fear was gone. I started running around and let him chase me. From that day on, we were inseparable while I stayed in Sólbakki. He followed me everywhere I went and kept me safe from the other dogs in the village. Lucky was the first friend I ever made, and ours was a true and unconditional friendship.

When we moved to Sólbakki, potatoes were grown there, and there were sheep and horses. In the past, there had been cows on the farm, and the cowshed was still there. There was a lot to explore in the countryside, and I experienced a lot of freedom. A huge space opened up for me. I was now able to go all over the village to look around, and Lucky followed me everywhere. It was all so exciting. I was curious and began to explore the surrounding farms. There was a big difference between this environment and our little garden on Ásvallagata. I enjoyed exploring the countryside.

Spiritual Awakening

Once we went on a long walk and came to a small field. "Let's rest," I said to Lucky, and lay down on the grass and looked up at the sky. The sky was a beautiful blue, and a few white clouds floated through the air. Lucky lay close against me, and we rested. "Lucky," I said, looking at him. He lifted his head. "Up there in the clouds are God and Jesus. They take care that no harm comes to us." Lucky howled low and laid his head down again. I felt like everything was eternal and I was eternal. I felt like I was floating up into the clouds, and I fell asleep there in the grass with Lucky by my side. When I woke up later, he was still lying next to me. "Let's head home," I said. We got up and walked back to the farm.

I slept in the same room as my great-grandfather from Hófgerði, and we spent a lot of time together. My great-grandmother had stayed behind in Reykjavík and had moved from Hófgerði to a small apartment in downtown Reykjavík. My great-grandfather and I talked a lot, and I was always asking questions about life and our existence. He always had time for me and was always teaching and guiding me.

During the year and a half we lived in Þykkvabær, my mother met another man who was born and raised there. Later, they decided that the three of us would move to Reykjavík and that one of my mother's brothers and his wife would take over the farm in Sólbakki. I was fortunate enough to spend the summers with my uncle and his wife until I got into my teenage years. The summers I spent in Þykkvabær are very precious to me, and I am very grateful for the time I got to spend there. I enjoyed myself there and experienced a lot of freedom.

We moved to Grettisgata 2 in Reykjavík, and it was my home until I was twelve years old. I started going to school in Austurbæjarskóli, which was in our neighborhood. The building seemed huge to me when I stood in front of it on my first day of school. I went to a class called DV, which stood for Dagný Valgeirsdóttir, the name of the teacher. She was my main teacher until I was twelve. She was a good teacher and was strict when she needed to be. I did well studying under her, and I liked it at school, although recess and the Christmas celebration were the most memorable moments from elementary school.

My maternal grandmother and her husband lived at Þingholtstræti 8B, which was within walking distance of our home. My great-grandfather, who had now moved from the country, and my great-grandmother lived at Miðstræti 3, which was also within walking distance of my home. They were all very dear to me and were always willing to help. I guess you could say I visited them over the years.

I was very fortunate to have so many grandparents around as a child. I always felt comfortable with older people; there was a certain calm and peace around them, and I enjoyed asking questions and learning. I kept asking questions about everything under the sun.

My great-grandmother was a very religious woman and believed in Jesus Christ and God. Although she rarely went to church, she had the Bible on her table and read it often. She taught me a lot about Jesus Christ and his life. I once asked in amazement, "How could they crucify such a good man? A man who healed people and helped others?" My great-grandmother looked at me and said, "Not everyone in this world is good." She emphasized the importance of saying prayers. I prayed every night, as I had done ever since my mother taught me the Lord's prayer on Ásvallagata.

My two grandmothers were both very religious and spiritual women. They often visited a medium together to get word from dead relatives. They also went to a medical medium to get cures for their ailments. During those years, they never discussed these things with me. "You'll understand when you grow up," they said when I asked about it. But I often listened and found it very interesting and exciting. For me, life after death was as normal as life itself.

Until I was twelve years old, I grew up in downtown Reykjavík. In those years, there were a lot of people downtown, and it was very lively. On Sundays at six in the evening, *Stundin okkar* was on TV, and back then it was the only children's program available. But I used to go to the movies at three in the afternoon on Sundays, and it was a great experience. I usually went to Gamla bíó, which was within walking distance of our home.

I played outdoors a lot, and when there was snow and frost, we used to skate on the pond in Reykjavík or Melavöllur or slide down Arnarhóll on our sleds. The boys and I played a lot of soccer on the campus grounds after school.

School life could at times be hard. There was teasing, skirmishes, fighting, and bullying. The teasing didn't affect me, and I didn't take it personally even though I was teased, but I had trouble handling fights and skirmishes. I tried my best to get out of the way because it didn't agree with me, and if I got into a fight, I felt bad for a long time afterward.

I sometimes felt anxious as Sunday went on. It was due to the school week ahead. Sometimes I got sick to my stomach and felt bad. I didn't tell anyone because I thought it was all normal, like catching a cold in winter. My anxiety would grow and bother me and be my companion for many years.

The Teenage Years

At the age of twelve, elementary school was over, as well as my time with my teacher Dagný. I had done well in school under her. She had a way of keeping me busy and studying. Then secondary school took over, where each teacher taught his or her own subject.

There were also changes in our home life that year, as my mother and stepfather divorced. My mother and I continued living on Grettisgata. This divorce affected me deeply. Soon after the divorce, we moved to Tungusel 10 in Breiðholt. Moving from downtown Reykjavík to Breiðholt was a big change. I decided to continue at Austubæjarskóli and finish the remaining three years of compulsory education. I commuted on the city buses.

The divorce and the move affected me greatly. I started doing poorly at school and studied much less than before. It was only many years later that I realized how deeply this divorce had touched me.

When I was in high school, I started looking into spirituality. I became interested in deciphering dreams, bought a book on the subject, and read it every morning to decipher the dreams of the past night. I found it exciting and interesting. I began looking at mysterious things that I found curious and that hadn't been settled in those days. I read a lot about the Bermuda Triangle and the pyramids of

Egypt. I began to wonder about the afterlife and what would happen when we left this Earth. The friends and acquaintances I talked to all had their own opinions. I believed that life went on after death but in a different form. Sometimes I would sit in the classroom contemplating life and existence, and I was often distracted from my classes. My interest in school and my studies had diminished, and as a teenager, it was a great struggle for me to wake up in the morning.

I stepped up my studies the last winter in high school and managed to graduate from Austurbæjarskóli with an average grade point average. For a long time afterward, I missed my classmates, as most of the class had stuck together from ages six to sixteen. One day we parted ways, and each headed off into life and started tackling the challenges that lay ahead.

When the deadline for applying to college had almost arrived, my mother asked, "Aren't you going to apply to college?"

I looked at her. "I suppose I should look into that."

"Educating yourself pays for itself many times over. Then you won't have to strive to earn every penny like I've had to and work from morning till evening just to make ends meet."

My mother always insisted that I would be educated. I felt the same way. I picked up a little manual I had received upon graduating from Austurbæjarskóli. It was on the country's high schools and what programs were available.

Spiritual Awakening

I sat at the kitchen table at home in Tungusel and flipped through the book many times. I had no idea what I wanted to do with my life or what path to take in my studies. After a while, I had decided and I got up and walked over to my mother, who was sitting in the living room. "I'm going to study business. I'll go to high school and then to the university."

My mother looked at me. "It's good to hear you've found what you're interested in."

"I think it suits me well. I'm going to write an application to send to Ármúli High School."

I started my business studies at Ármúli in the fall of 1986, and in my memory, they mostly consisted of bookkeeping and typing. From the very beginning, I studied half-heartedly. I knew few people at school and often thought of my schoolmates from Austurbæjarskóli, whom I often missed. "Where are they all now?" I often thought to myself. There were often gaps in the timetable, with an hour or two between classes. It was a long time to wait, and I didn't have the discipline to sit down in the library and study; sometimes, I simply decided to go home.

However, I made it through the first semester and finished with an average grade. I started having anxiety before exams and often felt bad the day before and in the morning on my way there. I was often dizzy with stress and distress when I walked into the exam room. This anxiety would follow me and only get worse throughout my

13

education. I didn't think much about spirituality at the time, but I always said my prayers at night.

When I started my new semester in January 1987, I had almost no interest in my studies. I thought to myself: "This is semester two of eight, followed by three to five years of college." It was an overwhelming thought; I couldn't imagine how I would get through it. Each day was akin to torture. I started being absent a lot from class, and by the end of January, I realized it was over. It was very difficult to tell my mother the news that I had quit school and was going to find a job. I knew the news would hurt her. When I had told her the news, I added reassuringly: "I will educate myself. I just need to figure out what to educate myself on. I promise."

A few days later, I had been hired at a small saltfish factory on the west side of Seltjarnarnes, near the lighthouse at Grótta. The foreman picked people up for work in a small van, and so that he could pick me up, I moved in with my grandparents, who were then living on Skólavörðustígur. It was hard work from eight in the morning to half past nine at night, seven days a week. It was a great adventure and experience. I got to know many good and interesting people there.

One older man and I immediately became great friends, and we talked a lot. I always remember he once said: "The people with money make slaves like us work all day so that we don't have the time or energy to think." I didn't understand it then, but I understood it years later.

Spiritual Awakening

He had worked with fish all his life and was good and could fillet fish quickly.

There was a lot of work there until spring, but when the season ended and summer came around, there was a lot less to do. So I decided to make a change and took a job as a handyman in construction that summer. Suddenly I got the urge to be a sailor and decided to do that during the autumn. I started looking for space on a fishing boat or trawler and contacted many captains but never got a positive reply. My mother advised me to find an education program that would suit me, so I began to wonder what I wanted to study while looking for a boat to work on.

I finally applied to study to become an electrician at Reykjavik Technical College, and shortly I received the answer that I was on a waiting list and would receive an answer at the end of August. Alongside construction, I continued to look for work at sea. Then it so happened that during the same week at the end of August, I got a positive response from the technical college that I could start my studies to become an electrician in early September, and one of the captains contacted me and offered me a place, saying that I could start in September. After some deliberation, I decided to start my studies at Reykjavík Technical College and gave up on my dream of being a sailor.

I liked the studies and found the profession interesting and exciting. I did well in the beginning, but in the latter part of the first semester, my interest and enthusiasm disappeared. I didn't take any exams during the semester, and I dropped out of school at the end of the year. I didn't feel at home doing anything. I was discouraged, and I lacked all structure in my life. In January 1988, I was in Bolungarvík during the fishing season and worked in saltfish processing until spring. It was a great experience. The winter was harsh with heavy snow, frost, and winds. I met different and interesting people there. I had begun to watch the people around me and think about them.

At that time, I again began to wonder about the meaning of life. "There must be something more than just work and toil," I thought to myself. Deep down, I felt that I now wanted something more and something bigger than working in a fishery, and I began to regret quitting my electrician studies. I still found it an exciting and interesting subject. "It was a mistake to drop out of the technical college," I thought to myself while I was shoveling salt from the floor of the saltfish factory into a giant bag.

There was an older man who regularly came to visit us at work and had coffee with us. He was not very fond of people from Reykjavík. During every visit, he said that they stole all the money from the rural people and left them in bitter poverty. I didn't know much about it and couldn't say much. He used to address me directly. "You people from the south," I often heard him say while looking at me sharply. It was uncomfortable, and I was often disturbed by those words.

Once when he addressed me like that, I calmly said to him, "I haven't stolen any money from anyone. I wouldn't be working here in boots and overalls shoveling salt if I'd stolen so much from you. I'd be somewhere else enjoying life."

He looked at me sharply for a long time and then said, smiling, "I like you, buddy."

After that, he stopped accusing me of stealing, and we became good friends.

My mother lived alone in Tungusel while I worked in the Westfjords. She had enrolled in senior education and finished her compulsory education with honors that spring. She had been only sixteen when I came into the world, so she had had to drop out of secondary school. I came home to Reykjavík in the spring, and during the summer, we discussed what would happen next. We finally decided to move to Sweden together, where her sister lived with her husband and children. They offered to help us get into the country and settled. We rented an apartment in Arlöv, just outside Malmö, and moved there in the autumn of 1988.

It was a strange feeling to suddenly be in a new environment, a new country, with a new language and a new culture. The apartment my mother and I had rented was within walking distance of my mother's sister and her family. They were a great help to us in getting started in a new country. We both started studying Swedish with the municipality and were in school for three hours a day. The studies went well, as Swedish is not so different from Icelandic. We were in a class with people from many countries—Vietnam, England, El Salvador, and

Yugoslavia, among others. We finished our studies in no time. Our teacher at school helped me get into high school, and I started at Pildam School in Malmö and went to a preparatory class for foreign students with a strong emphasis on Swedish among other subjects. The funding my mother had expected for her studies didn't come through, so she went to work.

My class included students from nineteen countries, and many of them were refugees who had experienced great hardships and wars in their home countries. I met a lot of these people and chatted with them often and for a long time when we had breaks from our studies. I was curious about these people's lives and their past. The most shocking story came from a young man from Iran. When he was a teenager, there was a war in his home country and a lot of conflict. One day when he came home from school, his family had all been shot dead—his parents, siblings, and grandmother. He collapsed from grief and had little choice but to leave his home and live on the street.

He dropped out of school and started working. He worked from morning till night, slept outside, and ate food he found in trash cans here and there. He saved everything he made for about a year and used the money to buy a false passport to get to Europe. He gathered food and supplies, as he was going to Europe on a multiweek trip with other people. A lot of people dropped off and gave up. Finally, he came to a high mountain range that he had to cross if he intended to make it all the way. Many people died on the mountain due to cold and wet weather and exhaustion. He persevered and finally made it to Europe.

"Now I'm here in Sweden with you," he said, smiling. I listened to the man and couldn't utter a word. He then went on to tell this story: "One time while I was walking in the city, there was a big firefight and I tried to flee for cover but was hit." Then he slid his pants down to his knees and pointed out two ugly scars on his thigh, one in the front and one in the back. "This is where the bullet went through," he said, looking up at me.

I was filled with great sympathy for the man, who was about twenty. He had no one, no family, and couldn't return to his home country at this time. "How are you feeling?" I asked.

"I'm so grateful to be here and to be able to educate myself," he said, smiling.

It dawned on me that I had grown up in a protected environment at home in Iceland without war and conflict and how much my family was worth. I couldn't bear to think of losing it all at once. I felt a pain in my chest at the thought. Then the school bell rang, and we walked into the school and to the classroom together. We talked a lot in our spare time, and he told me many stories about his home country, and I told him about Iceland and my childhood.

Studying at the Pildan School and getting to know all these different people who had a lot to share about their home countries was a great experience for me. I learned a lot from that alone.

My mother met an Icelandic man in Sweden. He moved in with us, and they started farming in the spring of 1989.

I missed my relatives and friends back home in Iceland and wrote many letters to them. I often thought of my maternal grandmother. I missed her and the time we had together a lot. I had visited her many times a week when I was in Iceland, and we would go on errands and drives together. I decided to visit Iceland in the summer of 1989 and stayed there for about a month. I got to stay with my grandparents that time, and we had a good time together.

One weekend while I was visiting Iceland, I met a woman, Halldóra Sæmundsdóttir, and we were together that weekend and liked each other. But we said goodbye on Sunday and didn't expect to see each other again.

I flew back home to Sweden, but this trip to Iceland had given me a strong desire to move back there. I felt how difficult it was to be away from relatives and friends for a long time. I discussed this with my mother and stepdad, and it was decided that we would all move back to Iceland. Then, in the autumn of 1989, we moved back to our apartment at Tungusel 10 in Reykjavík.

My time in Sweden was an adventure and a great experience. I met a lot of people and experienced a different culture.

The Student Years

I got a job at a fish-processing plant in the fall, and in October I met Halldóra again and we began a relationship. She lived in Akranes and had three children from her previous marriage. I lived in Reykjavík with my mother and stepfather, and I often went to Akranes on weekends. This is how life went that winter.

One day I was standing in boots and overalls in the cold freezer plant, threading string through cod heads, some of which had started to smell bad, and thought to myself, "I'm not going to spend my life here. I'd rather enroll in the technical college and continue my studies to become an electrician." That I did, and I started at the technical college in the fall of 1990. I was interested in the studies and did well. I went to Akranes on weekends.

I took three semesters at the technical college in Reykjavík but then moved to Akranes to live with Halldóra and her children. In January 1992, I started studying at Fjölbrautarskóli Vesturland. I graduated as an electrician around Christmas 1993. The master electrician I had been working for while studying told me that there was a big downturn and that he couldn't promise me much work after school. He encouraged me to continue my studies and aim for a technical course.

I researched the available options after the electrician course. What was available was industrial technology, which was a two-year program, and then engineering, which lasted three and a half years. In those days, engineering studies were only partially taught in Iceland: the first part was taught in Iceland, then the studies had to be completed abroad. Most students went to the technical school in Odense in Denmark, as that school collaborated with the Technical School of Iceland. At first, I leaned toward industrial technology, as I had little interest in moving abroad again. One of my teachers at Akranes had just graduated in electrical engineering from Odense, and we talked a lot about the program and what paths were available. I asked many questions. After these conversations, I became more and more interested in engineering.

Halldóra was willing to come with me to Denmark, so I applied for preparatory studies at the Technical School of Iceland, which was a technical education program for people from the trades that provided access to university and other technical studies. In January 1994, I started the preparatory studies at the technical school in Reykjavík. I stayed with my mother and stepfather on weekdays but traveled to Akranes on weekends. My mother and stepfather had moved to a small single-family home on Vesturbraut in Hafnarfjörður.

The studies were demanding, and I studied at school at night with several other students. Then, one Sunday, I was studying alone in the classroom and decided to take a break and go down to the library to look around. There I found a magazine stand with brochures from various schools

Spiritual Awakening

around the world. I found a big brochure from the University of Aalborg, which I took with me to the classroom. I soon saw that this was an exciting option because there would be the possibility of studying engineering after the technical studies if everything went well. I called Halldóra and asked if she wanted to come with me to Aalborg instead of Odense, and she right away she said, "Absolutely," but then added, "Where is that?" So we decided to move to Aalborg in the fall of 1995. I graduated from my technical studies at the Technical School of Iceland in the spring of 1995 after completing my apprenticeship as an electrician.

We decided that I would be alone in Aalborg for the first year. Her youngest son was finishing his compulsory education in Akranes, and after that, he and Halldóra would move to Aalborg in the spring of 1996. I got a room in a dormitory called Limfjords Kollegium on Bakkegårdsvej. My room was twelve square meters, with a private toilet and shower and a shared kitchen and dining room. Halldóra and I went to Aalborg in early August 1995, and it was a great adventure. We spent the month of August together in Aalborg, but then she went back to Iceland and I was left alone to start my studies in electrical engineering at the University of Aalborg. I had studied Danish in Iceland since I was eleven and thought that I was well prepared in Danish to start a new life on Danish soil.

On the first day of school, I arrived at a large hall at the school where all the new students were gathered. The headmaster gave a speech and welcomed us. He began his speech, saying very calmly, "Velkommen til Aalborg Universitet . . ." Then the speech started in earnest, and I didn't understand a word after the first sentence.

It was a big shock, and not what I had expected. I had thought I was better at Danish. "How can this work out if I don't understand anything?" I thought to myself. I went home to the dormitory and was gripped by great anxiety. Now Halldóra had gone back to Iceland, and I was lonely. The thought popped into my head to pack up and go back home to Iceland, but I decided to tough it out. The first day of class was the next day. I had a lot of anxiety later in the day and had trouble sleeping. From then on, anxiety plagued me more and more.

I rode my new bike, which Halldóra and I had bought a few days before, to school the next morning. All the first-year students were gathered in a large hall, where we were then sorted into groups. Six students were put in each group to work on a small project for one month. Next, each student's name was called, followed by a classroom number. I listened carefully for my name and room number. Finally, I heard it called, along with a room number I understood. I found the classroom down the hall, and when I got there, five Danes were sitting at a table and had started talking. I greeted them and introduced myself as I stood in the doorway. Then I took a seat at the table and watched.

I understood little of what was going on. I was anxious and lost my concentration as a result. I understood that they were talking about going to get pizza, and I took it to mean that after this first day together we would go to a restaurant and eat together. When they asked me about something, I just shrugged and felt like a fool. Suddenly, they packed up, got up, and went their separate ways. I hadn't understood where we were going, so I decided to follow one of the boys. We walked down the steps and to the front door, and I followed him to where he kept his bike, but mine was in a completely different spot. While he was placing the bag on the carrier and unlocking the wheels, he turned to me and asked me in Danish, "Why are you standing there?" I managed to tell him in broken Danish that I'd thought we were going to eat together after school. He smiled and said it was just an idea of something fun to do later. Then he rode away, and I was left alone, embarrassed.

I did not feel well. I was filled with anxiety and hopelessness. I couldn't imagine how I could start a demanding course of study on top of this. I rode slowly home and thought about what to do. "I can't give up now," I thought to myself, and started thinking about all the Icelanders who had come here before me and made it over this threshold. I decided to persevere and continue.

There was a phone in the room in the dormitory, and Halldóra and I spoke often during my first days at school. I needed support, and she encouraged me. During those first days, I sometimes felt sick from anxiety when cycling to school in the morning. That's how the first month passed, and at the end of it the group completed the project. Then we were arranged into a new group of six who were supposed to work on a project together until Christmas. I went to a new group with completely different students, and they were all Danes. The assignment we were given was to investigate the differences between publishing newspapers online and publishing them in print. The internet was new at the time, so it was all new and exciting.

As the fall progressed, I began to understand more and was now able to hold small conversations with my fellow students. Halldóra and I had decided that she would move out to live with me after Christmas and that her son would be in the care of his father until next spring. Thus, we applied for a larger apartment that would suit us, and in November we got a two-room apartment at the C.W. Obel dormitory. Halldóra came in November, and we moved our things together to the new apartment. Then she went back to Iceland.

When December arrived, I started counting down the days until Christmas. I had bought a plane ticket to Iceland just before Christmas and planned to spend Christmas there with Halldóra and the children and my friends and relatives. Halldóra and I then planned to fly back out together after Christmas.

The autumn exams were held at the beginning of January. I was very anxious before the tests, and the anxiety only increased as the exams drew closer. I lost my appetite, lost a lot of weight during the exams, and had trouble sleeping. This anxiety continued throughout the course and worsened year by year. I often felt sick on my way to exams, but I felt a great sense of relief when the exams were over

Spiritual Awakening

and I could breathe for a while. At the start of my studies, I often doubted myself and was not at all sure that I would be able to finish them. I had made up my mind that there would be exams that I would not pass. One of my acquaintances often comforted me and said, "If we fail, so will many others." It assuaged my concerns a little bit.

Halldóra and I were both in Denmark from the beginning of the year until the summer of 1996, when our youngest son moved out to live with us. The older son did not want to move to Denmark at all and remained in Iceland. Her eldest daughter had moved out on her own in Iceland. Our son had enrolled in baking studies in Aalborg. We found an Icelandic teacher who taught baking and had lived in Denmark for many years who was going to help him with his studies. Our son experienced the same thing I had with the language and wanted to move back home to Iceland. I helped him over this threshold, and he soon started to feel comfortable in Denmark.

We were in Denmark in the summer and then went to Iceland during Christmas and the New Year. There was great anticipation throughout the month of December to get home to see our relatives and friends. Communication in those days consisted of letters and limited phone calls. It was expensive to call internationally, and we didn't have a lot of money. We usually flew to Iceland around December 20 and stayed until the end of the year. Exams started in January.

While we lived in Aalborg, Halldóra and I tried to have another child. But after three early miscarriages, we

27

stopped trying. It was accompanied by more sadness and loss than I had realized.

Our years in Aalborg were fun and rewarding. Moving to another country, learning the language, and experiencing a different culture than the one you were brought up with is equivalent to university studies. Halldóra and I agree that, when we look back, these five years in Denmark were some of our best.

During those years, I didn't know how to enjoy the moment. Most of the time, I was thinking about the future and what would happen after my studies. Where would I get a job, and where would we live? So you can say that part of this time passed me by. It wasn't until much later that I learned to be in the moment and enjoy life to the fullest.

We often went for long walks around Aalborg, both in our neighborhood and around the dormitory and the university campus, as well as in central Aalborg on weekends. The walks helped me clear my mind and ward off the anxiety that frequently came up. My stepson and I often went for long walks together and supported each other. I stopped riding my bike to school and started walking back and forth instead. It took me about twenty-five minutes to walk one way. I was wide awake when I got to school, and I had already cleared my mind when I got home.

From the beginning, we were determined to continue living in Denmark after my studies ended. It was then, during the second half of my studies, that I started

Spiritual Awakening

opening up to the possibility of moving back to Iceland after graduation. Halldóra was not open to that and preferred to stay in Denmark. My desire to move to Iceland started to get stronger and stronger, and about a year after my studies began, I started to look at job opportunities in Iceland. I made a list of possible companies and engineering firms. Once again, I had my mind set far in the future.

In February 2000, my mother contacted me and told me that the US military base in Keflavík was advertising for an electrical engineer who should start working there in the summer. I decided to apply and see what would happen, and I stated in the application that I would graduate in June that year and could subsequently start working. I didn't get any response to the application, so I thought it wouldn't work out. Then, in May, I received a call from the military's personnel department, which explained the job and its salary and benefits. As the interview progressed, I realized they were offering me the job. I hadn't had any interviews as I had expected to before being hired. I got to talk to the head of the engineering department, who explained to me in more detail what the job was about. These were various engineering designs in the defense area and in the area of Keflavík Airport. This sounded very exciting.

"Will you manage to graduate?" the department head finally asked me.

"I don't expect otherwise," I replied.

Ragnar Viktor Karlsson

"We'll see you in the summer—that is, if you are interested in the job."

I got back in touch with the personnel department, and they asked me if I wanted the job. I wrote down for Halldóra what it was that I was talking about on the phone, and she whispered to me, "Say yes, and let's go." I accepted the job and signed a contract a few days later by email.

I graduated as an electrical engineer from the University of Aalborg at the end of June 2000. It was a great joy and a moment of victory for me to have reached this stage with the kind help of my wife Halldóra and my relatives and friends. My parents had come along with relatives and friends to Aalborg to congratulate me on graduation day. When the headmaster gave the farewell speech to those of us who were graduating, I remembered the first speech he had given five years before, when I hadn't understood anything that was going on. I smiled to myself and thought about how much had changed since then. Then I had been full of anxiety and fear, but now I understood every word of the speech and was full of joy and happiness. I had an exciting time ahead of me, with new tasks and challenges.

Life after My Studies

Halldóra and I moved to Iceland in the summer of 2000, but our youngest son stayed on in Denmark and worked as a baker. We bought an apartment in Laugardalur, and Halldóra got a job in Reykjavík, while I started working for the US military in Keflavík. In our free time, we traveled around Iceland and went on many day trips as well as weekend trips. During the summer vacations, we took longer trips, traveling with a small tent and sleeping bag around one area each summer. We often slept in the car if we didn't feel like pitching the tent. It was a great adventure to experience Iceland after such a long absence. I experienced the colors so strongly—the grass was dark green, and the sky was dark blue. The mountains against the sky were majestic and breathtaking. The light in Iceland was also different than in Denmark.

I liked my job and had a lot of ambition to do well at it. The projects were all different. There were about twenty of us Icelandic employees who worked in the engineering department.

In 2002, we bought a single-family home in Álftanes, a house that needed renovation, and we were ready to tackle it. The house had a beautiful view of Reykjavík, and the plot of land reached down to the sea. "This will be our future home," I thought to myself as I stood looking out the living room window at the still sea. Slowly we started fixing and renovating the house.

When I had been working for the US military for about three years, the rumor started to spread that it was planning to significantly reduce its activities in Iceland or even close the base and leave Iceland. It was a big shock to hear this news, and great anxiety gripped me. The anxiety I had been suffering from during my studies had returned. "If I lose my job, I'll lose my salary and lose my home," I thought, and started imagining the worst. "This isn't what I need now that everything is going so well," I thought to myself. Then the rumors began to appear in the Icelandic media, which only added to the anxiety. I had started to feel sad and withdrew a lot from other people.

What had started as gossip became reality when mass layoffs were announced to the staff. Some of my coworkers were laid off, and the group started to thin out. A little later, when everything was becoming balanced again, there was another round of layoffs. A lot of tension, anxiety, and fear accompanied this period. So it went, until only a few of us were left in the engineering department. The light-hearted, good working spirit that prevailed there when I had come to work a few years earlier had now disappeared, and a lot of tension and uncertainty was in the air.

In May 2006, I sat down to watch the news one evening, and the first news item was that the military would leave Iceland in September that year and the base would be closed. In an instant, I felt a pain in my chest, and a great fear gripped me. "What do I do now?" I thought to myself. It was a huge shock that I didn't know how to handle. The atmosphere at work the next day was strange. Few managed to concentrate on the tasks; instead, people were discussing the previous day's news and reviewing the situation. The world and environment in which we had lived and worked was disappearing. This was a big blow to the workers, many of whom had worked there for many years and knew little else. "I'm young and I'm educated, and many paths are open to me," I thought to myself to motivate myself and inspire hope.

In less than two weeks, I got a job at an engineering firm in Hafnarfjörður, a few minutes' drive from our home. It was difficult to start work in a new place. I was not happy with having to quit Keflavík, and I missed my colleagues from there, as we had been a very close-knit group, like a family.

The new job went well, and I gradually adapted to the new situation. There was a lot to do, and the days were long and hard. At the same time, Halldóra and I were renovating our home in Álftanes. We worked on it in the evenings and on weekends alongside other work. We were building a home for the future, and we felt good in Álftanes and in our house there.

We were four electricians at the new workplace, working on wiring designs for all types of buildings. The construction market was booming, and there was lots of work. Things developed in such a way that I began working a lot with one of the electricians, and we developed a close

33

relationship. One day, having gone out to the site together, as we often did to help the contractors, on the way home I said, "It would be nice to start a company that offers electrical wiring design and advice and then sell lights and equipment. Offer people and companies complete solutions so they don't have to go to so many places."

My colleague looked at me, smiled, and said, "I've had this idea in my head for a long time."

With those words, the ball started rolling. Things happened quickly. We were now both consumed by the idea and began to lay the groundwork and plan. We met in the evenings to shape the activities and the company and what we intended to offer. We looked for foreign suppliers of lights and electrical materials. After a lot of work and planning, we decided to look for suitable premises for a lighting and electrical shop, together with an electrical design office. In the end, we bought a commercial building in Hamraborg, Kópavogur. It needed to be renovated and adapted to our operations. We took a bank loan to finance the project.

It was a heavy moment when we both walked into our boss's office and informed him that we were going to start our own company and quit our jobs. This went down very badly with the owners of the engineering office, and there certainly wasn't any farewell party held for us when we left our jobs. I felt terrible about how it had ended because it was a good place to work and the owners were excellent bosses who took care of the staff in every way.

Spiritual Awakening

At the beginning of January 2008, we started working on the renovation of the premises and worked twelve to fourteen hours a day, every day of the week, for about two months. At that moment, I began to doubt whether it was the right decision to start the company, but there was no turning back. The anxiety started to plague me again, and I started to fear what would happen if this didn't work out.

We talked a lot during the construction. It soon became clear that we were both interested in spiritual matters, and we began to discuss the meaning of life and the possibility of life after death. I told him that I believe that we live many times here on Earth and get to experience different things in each life to grow and improve. If we look at the people around us, they are so different: some become famous and rich, while others are isolated and poor. Then there are those who are born with disabilities, either physical or mental. We can't be given just one chance when people's living conditions and lives are so different. "Where is the fairness in that?" I asked, and he looked at me for a long time and said, "You must have read *The Handbook of Michael*, because everything you are saying is in it."

I wondered about this. "I've never heard of that book," I replied, intrigued. I hadn't read any books on spirituality at the time. During our conversation, a spark ignited something within me, and I found it very interesting. I was happy to have finally met someone who was interested in spiritual matters. "Tell me more about this book," I said. I had become excited. "Who is Michael? What is the book about?" I had a lot of questions and was eager to know more.

He started telling me about the book. "Michael is a family of about a thousand souls who all have completed their earthly lives and have united as one entity. The earthly experiences of all the souls have now become one whole."

I listened in amazement and said, "There is a lot of information and experience in there."

"Absolutely," he replied, and continued, "Then there are mediums that have communicated information from Michael, and this book was written that way. They call themselves casual forces and bring information down to Earth to teach and educate and help other souls who are here on Earth."

I stared at him in wonder, listening to every word. I found it so interesting. Although I was hearing this for the first time in my life, it all felt so familiar. Sometimes I felt like it was a kind of recap of something I knew from a long time ago.

He went on to tell me about the book. "The soul begins as an infant soul and lives about two hundred times here on Earth on average. Sometimes less and sometimes more—it depends on how the soul develops. But then the soul becomes an old soul, and eventually it completes all its earthly lives and ceases to be embodied on Earth."

I smiled and said, "I'm an old soul, definitely on my last life."

He replied, "Me, too." Then he added, "Who doesn't want to finish up here on Earth as soon as possible?"

We talked a lot about spirituality, but he had read the book many times and applied these teachings in his life and relationships with other people. "I need to find this book and read it," I said, and was very thirsty for more knowledge. A new world and new dimensions had opened up to me. I had started a spiritual journey and was eager to know more.

"I doubt that you will find the book in most bookstores, but you should find it in an antiquarian bookstore."

I went to Kolaportið in Reykjavík and found an antiquarian bookseller sitting on a chair among thousands of books, on shelves all around and lying in piles on many tables. I walked up to the man and asked, "Do you have *The Handbook of Michael?*"

He looked at me thoughtfully for a moment, then turned around in his chair and pointed with one hand to a bookshelf behind him. "It's there on the second shelf."

I quickly walked to the shelf and immediately found the book, and on the book cover it said "Handbook of Michael." I felt like I had found a treasure. "Finally," I thought to myself, "Finally, I have the book." I immediately started flipping through the book as I stood by the shelf. "I have to get home to read," I thought to myself. Then I went to the man, paid for the book, and headed home.

My First Steps in Spiritual

Matters

After much work in renovating the property in which we had invested, we opened the company at the beginning of March 2008. We were busy from the start, and many projects arrived. Although the business started out well, there were great disturbances within me. I sometimes feared for my income and livelihood. Now we had to make sure we could afford the next salary payment and run the company. Although I felt good on most days, there were other days when anxiety and fear took control and I experienced great discomfort.

Along with running the business, I had my mind on spiritual matters, which I discussed with my business partner when we had a break from our work. I thought of little else, and being overwhelmed by spiritual teachings, I had many burning questions on my mind. I greatly desired more and more knowledge and wanted to know who I was and what my place was in all this. These spiritual matters seemed so familiar to me, and I felt as if I was discovering the final pieces in the puzzle of life. "How can you live without this knowledge?" I thought to myself.

I read about the soul, that we are eternal souls who lived many lives here on Earth and passed from one age to another. The soul is a particle of light that comes from

God. Its incarnation begins on Earth, and it lives an average of about two hundred lives before finally graduating from the earthly school. Then we become spiritual, and the soul is finally reunited with God, taking with it the experiences it acquired here on Earth. The purpose is to experience and deal with different earthly challenges, to experience being an individual in a body separated from God's energy. The experience of each soul is the experience of the whole.

When the soul begins the process on Earth, it is at an age called infancy. These souls have a strong connection with nature and are satisfied fulfilling the basic human needs. They prefer to live in remote places away from complex societies. Simplicity suits these souls best. They prefer to live near the equator, where weather variations are few and the climate is stable. The souls often live in groups but form few emotional bonds with others. They don't thrive in cities and technological societies. When they live in such conditions, they run the risk of becoming career criminals and being outcasts. The infant souls enjoy living primitively in the forest and in more remote places, which are where they find peace.

The soul lives many lives in each age. It completes the developmental stages of one age before moving on to the next age. The process is similar to that of school, where one must finish first grade before advancing to second grade.

I was fascinated by these teachings, as I thought they aligned very well with life and people here on Earth.

Spiritual Awakening

When the soul has completed its lives in infancy, it becomes a baby soul. At this age, the soul begins to adjust to being in communion with others. It feels good about having rules to follow and having discipline—like a small child who needs guidance, discipline, and security from its parents. These souls have a hard time changing their opinions and steadfastly hold on to them instead. They tend to use a lot of physical violence. The baby souls often live in difficult and challenging situations, and each of their lives is short. They experience natural disasters, famines, and wars because they choose countries where these things are possible. They often choose to live in countries with strong military and police rule. Africa and the Middle East are good examples of places where these souls choose to live.

After baby soul age, the soul transitions to the young age, which can be compared to a young person who is full of energy and can conquer the world. These souls are lively and are the driving force in the world. They are full of ideas and have the energy to implement them. They see life as a challenge and a competition. The goal of the competition is often to be the richest and most famous, which they feel is a sign of success in life. Sometimes the competitive spirit is so great that they tread on others to achieve their goals. They are convinced that they live one life here on Earth and that nothing happens after that. Therefore, they are terrified of growing old and dying, as for them death is the end of everything. Career and financial success come first, while family and friends are secondary priorities. Religion

41

and spirituality are nonsense and a waste of time in the eyes of these souls. To them, the body and the mind are all that is.

Although our business was off to a good start, I lacked financial stability and security, and I feared for my income: "Would we be able to afford the salary payments at the end of the month? What happens if we can't?" Such thoughts came to mind regularly. But we often had time to chat, and we talked a lot about spiritual matters and exchanged opinions and speculations about life and our existence. Talking about these things always calmed me down, and then the anxiety went away. I continued to study spirituality whenever the opportunity presented itself.

The next age of the soul is the mature age, when the soul begins to awaken to who it is. This age can be compared to a spiritual awakening. Communication with other people and social life are now more important than the fame and fortune that used to prevail. Family is important, as is spending time with relatives and friends. This age is mentally demanding for the individual, and great internal conflicts often take place, similar to the conflicts that occur at the beginning of a spiritual awakening. The Nordic countries, where relationships and family life come first, are a good example of an area with mature souls.

The last age is old age, at which point the soul has become aware that it is part of something bigger and that death is not the end. The soul spends more time alone, enjoying nature and gardens. It enjoys living in peace.

Spiritual Awakening

Worldly things are less important, and the soul is content and economical. It is not as energetic as the young soul and is more relaxed. The soul starts looking for answers about spiritual issues that are often an important part of its life. It knows that there is life after death and, therefore, rarely fears death.

Finally, when the soul has completed all its lives here on Earth, it joins its family of souls in the astral plane. Each soul family has about one thousand souls. When all the souls have completed their lives and the whole family is united as one, the soul family goes up to the casual plane, where the experiences of all the souls are combined into one whole. Thus, the experience of each individual is the experience of the whole.

In the very spring after we opened our company, news began to emerge about turmoil in the financial markets and that a storm was brewing. The Icelandic government announced that there was nothing to fear. Yet the news and surrounding discussions did not reduce my anxiety, and I often felt bad. I often had difficulty sleeping and came to work having slept poorly or very little. But when we were assigned some big projects, I was filled with optimism and my worries subsided.

Although the company was off to a good start, I was beginning to feel that my stay there was temporary. Without being able to explain the feeling in any detail, I simply didn't see myself staying with the company for a long time.

I continued to study spirituality and began to look at the seven soul roles. Each soul has two roles and can switch between them at will. The soul roles are the same throughout all the soul's life here on Earth. They are our basic structure and determine how we approach things and our challenges. The roles are as follows: servant and priest; artist and storyteller; warrior and king; and, finally, scholar. The servant and the priest are inspirational roles and are brothers. These roles inspire others and help them when needed. The servant prefers to work behind the scenes and keep a low profile, while the priest has leadership skills and speaks to and reaches the masses. In the same way, the artist and the storyteller are brothers. They are creative roles. The artist is an art creator and inventor, while the storyteller is an actor. The warrior and the king are active roles, where the warrior is a hard worker and the king is a ruler. Finally there's the scholar, who is a thinker. It's a neutral role and stands alone. These roles are clearly expressed in the bearing and behavior of the individual.

It gives the servant fulfillment to be able to help others and provide assistance. He is extremely organized, and everything around him is in order.

The priest has an overview of life, is extremely sensitive, and has strong intuition. He senses what will happen. He inspires others and is a good leader.

The artist is the inventor and the creator. He has a lively imagination and is full of ideas. He is sensitive and can therefore laugh and cry easily.

Spiritual Awakening

The storyteller is a lively person and views life as a game. He is the actor and narrator and enjoys himself on stage. He is inquisitive and curious and enjoys telling stories and making others happy.

The warrior is organized and finishes the job before it even begins. He protects his family and friends. He is a trusted friend. He lives a disciplined and selfless life. He is very down-to-earth and has no interest in spiritual matters. However, this attitude changes when the soul is well into the old phase.

The king has an overview of things and enjoys managing and planning. Like the warrior, he is a down-to-earth and loyal friend. He tends to be arrogant.

Finally there's the scholar. He enjoys learning, collecting, and absorbing information in different ways. He has little need to share his knowledge with others. He is curious, always wanting to know more and how everything works. All the knowledge and experience he acquires in life become useful to the whole when the souls are finally united.

I now began to find my roles. I quickly discovered that I was a scholar and that there was no doubt about it. It seemed clear to me. Then there was the second role. I struggled to discover what that was and pondered on it for a long time. I was starting to lean toward the king, but I felt it was unlikely as only 1 to 2 percent of souls are in this role. But after taking a closer look and delving deeper into myself, my behavior, and my approach to life, I became even more convinced that it was the right role. Finally, I was certain of it. My roles are scholar and king.

"I wish I had discovered this knowledge earlier in my life. How can you live without it?" I thought to myself after finding my soul roles. At that time, spiritual matters for me were only about knowledge. I desperately wanted to know more about myself, the soul, life, and life after death.

When I had knowledge about the soul's age and roles, a fun and exciting time began as I started to look at and think about the soul roles of my family, relatives, and friends. In most cases, the roles of my family were easy to find, but discovering my own roles could be trickier. I knew immediately that Halldóra was an artist; she was often dressed in colorful clothes, which is a characteristic of artists, but I did not find the second role. She can easily manage things and bring order to chaos, so I was leaning toward her being a king like me. I was also sure that my mother and grandmother were artists; they both did a lot of needlework and knitting. I was so fascinated by this that when I met other people, I began to wonder about their roles.

The storm in the financial markets continued brewing, and the mood in the country had become heavy. This added to my anxiety and fear. We didn't notice it in our business; there was plenty to do, and many projects arrived. The nation's ministers were often abroad and not here to answer for these issues. "I suppose they are looking for funds to be able to react if the worst scenarios came true," I thought to myself and tried to suppress my fear and

Spiritual Awakening

anxiety. We had a beautiful view of Fossvogur and Esjan from the windows where we sat, designing and drawing plans for electrical systems for buildings.

I continued to examine spirituality and started looking into personality and how it is composed and differs from life to life. For the soul to experience different things in its different lives, the personality changes from life to life and is the dominant factor in what the soul experiences. Are you forward, shameless, greedy, hardworking, or reserved? All this lies within the personality. Something I noticed in particular was that one part of the personality was called the main obstacle. This is a kind of obstacle on our journey and development. The task is then to become aware of this obstacle and overcome it. This will ease the path of life and speed up spiritual development. "How can you overcome this obstacle if you don't know it's there?" I thought to myself. Thus, it's important that as many people as possible know about these things and manage to use this knowledge to make life easier.

There are seven main obstacles, and every person has one. Each obstacle also has a positive pole. The obstacles are as follows: self-deprecation, arrogance, self-destruction, greed, martyrdom, impatience, and stubbornness. The root cause and common denominator of all these obstacles is fear.

A self-deprecating person fears making mistakes and feeling worthless, and he doubts himself. The positive pole of low self-esteem is modesty. Arrogance is the fear of being judged and not wanting to be seen as a weak point.

He who is arrogant is also proud. Self-destruction creates fear of the meaninglessness of life and of not being able to do anything about it. A greedy person fears scarcity and thus begins to accumulate what he is afraid of lacking in the future. The martyr fears becoming a victim in life. An impatient person fears missing out and being late. The stubborn one fears all changes. All this fear is an illusion created in the mind within us and therefore needs to be dealt with there.

I knew in my heart that somewhere there were mediums who could channel information and teaching from the casual plane. "There must be a lot of knowledge and information in a unity of souls, where the experiences of one thousand souls have been gathered, and each soul has lived an average of two hundred times here on Earth," I thought to myself. The scholar was fascinated by the thought of accessing such a collection of information in one place. I began to wonder if it was possible to find a medium somewhere in the world who could channel such things to me. "Where should I look?" I thought to myself. "It must be possible."

The Spiritual Mentor

Spirituality was now a big part of my life, and I was thinking about it all the time. "It is a privilege to have this information and be able to use it in everyday life and in communication with others," I thought to myself. This knowledge gave me a deeper understanding of people and the differences in their behavior. I stopped judging others and became more tolerant toward them.

One day when I was at work, I said to my partner, "It would be nice to find a medium who can channel this spiritual knowledge and thus give me access to all this knowledge."

My partner looked at me. "It's possible," he replied. "I know of a woman I went to many years ago. She channels Ásgeir, who is in the casual plane, a unity of a thousand souls."

I tensed up. "Is Ásgeir a family of one thousand souls?"

He smiled and said, "Yes, it is."

I interjected, "Can you ask anything you want?"

"Anything you want to know: the soul roles, soul age, and whatever. They are like an encyclopedia," he replied.

"Do you have this woman's phone number? Where does she live?" I asked anxiously. This was something I had to look into more closely. "I have to find this woman and get to her."

My partner looked at me and said, "I have her phone number somewhere at home. I'll see if I can find it tonight."

"Please do," I replied excitedly. The first thing I said to my partner the next morning was, "Do you have the phone number? Did you find it?"

He looked at me, disappointment etching his face. "No, I couldn't find it anywhere."

"Can you keep looking?" I asked eagerly.

"I'll continue looking when I get home tonight."

For the next two weeks, the mornings passed like this: I would ask if he had found the number, but alas, no number. Finally, one morning when we were drinking our coffee to prepare ourselves for the day's work, he said with a smile, "I have good news."

I interjected, "Well, tell me."

He took out a small note and handed it to me, saying, "I found the number last night. It's right here on this piece of paper."

I smiled and excitedly took the paper and unfolded it. Written on the paper were "Guðbjörg" and a phone number under the name. I happily looked at my partner and said, "Thank you so much for this. I'll call today and make an appointment."

Spiritual Awakening

He looked at me and said, "Can't I come with you? We can both be with her at the same time. She is used to receiving more than one at a time."

I thought this was a good idea. "Sure. It will be exciting. I'll call her around noon," I replied and placed the note on my desk.

Finally noon arrived, and we ate and had a cup of coffee afterward. "Well," I said as I stood up. "It's time. I'll call her now."

My partner looked at me and said, "Exciting. Good luck."

I took the piece of paper, left the room, and placed the paper in front of me. I felt excited, with a mixture of anticipation and mild anxiety. I typed her number into the phone, and it rang. Finally there was an answer. It was a soft and comfortable female voice that answered, "Guðbjörg."

"Hello, this is Viktor," I said softly and shyly. "I have been reading *The Handbook of Michael* on the soul age and soul roles, and I am looking for a medium who can impart such information and knowledge to me. My business partner directed me to you and gave me your phone number."

She listened to me and then replied, "I have been channeling these teachings for over twenty years, and they are always equally exciting. I work with and channel Ásgeir, who are mostly storytellers' souls and priests' souls but

51

have the same information as Michael. You would enjoy chatting with Ásgeir. I go into a trance when I channel them, so it's like you're talking to them directly."

The shyness was gone, and I was filled with great anticipation and excitement. This was fascinating. "Can I ask them questions when I'm with you? For example, what my soul roles and age are?"

"You can ask them anything, and they'll answer. It is best to have concise questions. Then you'll get concise answers."

"This sounds very exciting," I replied.

She added, "It will be nice to have you with us."

"Can my partner join?" I asked.

"That's even better," answered Guðbjörg.

"What roles are you in?" I asked.

"I am a storyteller and an artist," she answered. After we had chatted for about an hour, she asked, "Can you come to my place on Thursday next week at two?"

Without thinking, I answered, "Yes, that's fine."

She wrote our names in a notebook and then said, "Now you are in my book. I look forward to seeing you." She hung up.

"That was amazing and interesting," I thought to myself. To be able to find such a medium in Iceland was more than I had hoped for. I felt like a child a week before

Spiritual Awakening

Christmas. I was filled with anticipation and expectation the whole week we waited for the appointment with Guðbjörg Sveinsdóttir.

Soon after we opened the store and the design studio, I could feel that business wasn't for me. I liked doing the designs, but the business part was not my forte. I felt guilty about buying a product at wholesale price and then having to mark it up and sell it to the customers for a higher price. Yet I knew deep down that the markup went toward running the store and paying our salaries. Once an elderly woman came into the store looking for light bulbs. We started talking, and I found the bulbs and put them on the counter. She began looking in her purse and did so for a long time.

"Did you forget your wallet?" I asked with a smile.

She looked up worriedly and said, "I don't think I have enough money with me. Oh, I thought I had it with me. I'll have to go home and get some more."

I slid the light bulbs over to her and said with a smile, "You can keep the bulbs."

She looked at me. "No, no, it's too much."

I pushed the light bulbs closer to her. "Just put them in your purse."

She became happy and smiled. "Well, friend, God bless you, and thank you very much. This saves me the steps."

I smiled. "Take care, and have a great day," I said, and the woman left the shop smiling. I followed her with my eyes and saw that she had a hard time walking. "Poor woman," I thought to myself.

I started preparing for the visit with Guðbjörg and began writing down questions on a piece of paper that I would bring with me. Question number one was, "What are my soul roles?" I then wrote the answer after the question. "A scholar and a king."

"Let's see if this fits," I thought to myself and added the next question: "What is my soul age?" I wrote, "An old soul." Then I decided to ask the same questions about Halldóra. When I had written this down, I thought to myself, "That's enough for now." My partner did the same, and we were ready for the meeting. I was very excited all week.

Finally the big day arrived. I started thinking about the meeting as soon as I woke up. "Do I have more questions?" I thought to myself as I drank my morning coffee in the kitchen at home. "I'll see what comes to mind during the meeting. Maybe I'll think of something." Time passed slowly this morning at work. I kept looking at the clock. We prepared a note to put in the shop window: "Temporarily closed. Opens at 16:00." I looked at the clock. "Well, it's time to get ready. We need to leave soon." We got up and went out to the car. My partner got behind the wheel and started the car. "Let's go to Hlíðarhjalli 10, top floor," I said with a smile. We had plenty of time and arrived early outside Guðbjörg's. "We are early. We can wait here for a few minutes." I was very excited and felt a mixture of anticipation and anxiety. I had been waiting for this meeting for a long time.

Spiritual Awakening

After a while, my partner said, "OK, it's time." We exited the car and slowly walked toward the beautiful apartment building. We walked into the lobby and read the names on the doorbell. I scanned all the names and finally I saw it: Guðbjörg Sveinsdóttir on the top floor. "Now it's do or die," I said with a smile as I rang the bell. A long time passed before we heard a sound on the intercom.

"Welcome, boys," Guðbjörg said and opened the door. We went past the door and entered a very neat stairwell. I could feel my heart beating faster and faster the higher we went. As soon as we reached the top floor, the door on the left side of the landing opened, and there Guðbjörg stood smiling. "Welcome to our place." Guðbjörg was a thin woman with light-blond hair and white eye-catching glasses. "Come inside," she said, and motioned for us to enter.

We took off our shoes and coats in the lobby and followed her into a bright hallway that led us directly into a spacious living room. She pointed to the couch in the living room and said, "Please take a seat." She sat down in a chair across from us, and there was a sofa table between us. I looked around the living room, which was beautiful, and there were beautiful pictures hanging on the walls. I saw a fireplace in one corner. You could walk onto the balcony from the living room.

I was kind of shy sitting there on the couch. I put the question papers and the pen down and looked at Guðbjörg. She looked us up and down as if scanning us with her eyes. There was silence for a while, but finally she said, "Do you want coffee?"

We both answered, "Yes, thank you. That would be most appreciated."

She stood up and said, "Make yourselves at home while I get coffee for us."

We looked at each other and smiled. I felt myself starting to calm down, and the anxiety and tension gradually decreased. I noticed that there were tissues on the table. "Do people cry a lot here?" I thought to myself. Then Guðbjörg came back into the living room, brought us coffee, and sat down in the chair and pulled it closer to the table. She took a sip and looked at us alternately. I found and sensed that something great and remarkable was about to happen, although I didn't realize what it was.

Guðbjörg asked us about our company and what we were selling. We told her what we did. For some time we sat there in silence. She looked at us alternately as if she was scanning and checking us. I felt an increasing sense of calm while sitting there and chatting with Guðbjörg. Then she began to explain how the meeting would take place and said at the end, "I want to tell you this so nothing will surprise you."

After we had chatted for almost an hour, she said, "Well, they are here. Ásgeir has arrived and is looking forward to chatting with you." She smiled and grabbed a blanket that she wrapped around herself. "I always feel cold when I do this," she said and took off her glasses, placing them on the table in front of her. I adjusted myself on the sofa and found the paper with my questions and pen. She closed her eyes and placed her hands on the arms of the chair. She began to clear her throat and pull her nose forcefully. Then she slowly exhaled through her mouth. I followed her closely and found everything exciting and interesting. I was filled with expectation and anticipation.

After a little while, she started clearing her throat and said, "Welcome, both of you." The voice had become rough and husky, and I could sense that it was Ásgeir talking to us and not Guðbjörg. Everything from her movements, the words she used, and her voice were now completely different from what I had seen while I was talking to Guðbjörg.

"Finally I'm in contact with Ásgeir," I thought to myself and excitedly followed everything that happened.

We both said hello at once, and Ásgeir continued: "It is our honor to welcome you and to be with you here today. We'll let you ask questions, and you can ask anything you want. Can we start with him?" Ásgeir asked, pointing to my partner.

"Of course," I answered and was a bit shy sitting there on the sofa. My partner asked about his roles.

"Let's get the information down," Ásgeir said. After a short silence, the information came. "You are an artist. How do you like that?"

My partner answered, "Just fine."

Ásgeir added, "It's beyond dispute." Then Ásgeir reviewed the artist's characteristics and finally said, "Are you satisfied with this?"

We looked at each other. "That's a description of me," my partner replied.

"Good," said Ásgeir. "And the second role . . ." After a long silence, he quickly added, "You're a priest."

My partner smiled. This was what he had thought and suspected. "It fits," he said.

Ásgeir now reviewed the features of the priest and finally said, "Do you recognize this description?"

My friend smiled. "That's me in a nutshell." My partner then asked about the soul role of his family members, relatives, and friends, and Ásgeir provided the roles of all of them. When about half an hour had passed, he said to my partner, "Can we turn to Viktor now?"

I adjusted myself on the couch and felt a mixture of a little anxiety and a lot of anticipation as my heart pounded in my chest. I had been waiting for this moment for a long time, and now it had finally arrived.

My partner replied, "Yes, I'm satisfied. Thank you."

In his chair, Ásgeir turned toward me slightly. "Welcome, Viktor. It's an honor to have you here with us. This is our first meeting."

I replied softly and shyly, "Thank you. That's right. I haven't been here before."

After a long silence, Ásgeir asked, "What would you like to chat about?"

I looked down at my piece of paper and answered, "I want to know my soul roles."

Ásgeir cleared his throat. "Let's get the information down here. You are very curious and love to explore," Ásgeir said half questioningly.

"Very right," I replied.

"It goes without saying that you are a scholar."

I underlined the previous role on the paper. It's what I had thought and written down. "That might be right," I replied.

Then Ásgeir described the scholar. He's inquisitive and curious and feels most comfortable pondering and researching things. He never talks too much and doesn't like sharing the information he has. He fulfills a neutral role and doesn't answer yes or no but maybe, it's possible, or it can be looked into. He wants to be sure and looks at matters from all angles before answering. He might be reading in the living room but knows exactly what everyone else in the house is doing. Finally, Ásgeir said, "This is the scholar."

I smiled, "That fits me perfectly. You're describing me." Before the meeting, I was pretty sure about this first role, but the second one I wasn't quite sure about. Now I was excited to hear what Ásgeir would say about that.

There was a bit of silence, but then Ásgeir said, "The second role is . . . it is . . ."

There was a long silence, and I was very excited. I looked down at the paper and read in silence: king. "Could that be right?" I thought to myself.

"You are a king," Ásgeir finally said. He added, "We very rarely meet kings here."

I underlined the second role on the paper, which was also correct.

Then Ásgeir continued: "The king is a born ruler, and he is best at managing and planning. He is a reliable friend, but if someone harms him or his family, he'll shun that person. The king gives expensive gifts and buys expensive things for himself. With his demeanor, he can shut people out so they don't want to be in the king's presence, but at the same time, he can open up and cause people to flock to him. Arrogance can be present under the surface, and for a long time, spiritual matters are just nonsense. This changes as the soul starts to age." After a brief silence, Ásgeir asked. "How do you feel about this?"

I smiled. "This is what I suspected, and this description fits me well."

"Do you have more questions?" asked Ásgeir.

"I want to know my soul age."

I hadn't finished saying the word when Ásgeir answered, "You're a very old soul. You don't have to come back to Earth any more than you want to."

Spiritual Awakening

This was a great relief to me because sometimes being here on Earth can be challenging. I always felt like I didn't fit into the pattern. "Can I ask about the roles of my wife Halldóra?"

"Absolutely," answered Ásgeir. He quickly said, "She is a priest and an artist like your friend here." Then Ásgeir added, "How do you feel about this?"

I answered, "I was pretty sure about the artist, but I had wondered about the other role for a long time. I was starting to think she was a king as she can be controlling and quickly brings order to the chaos."

Ásgeir smiled. "No, you can't have two kings together. There is only one king in each palace. The controlling aspect and her oversight come from her priest."

I found it all fascinating and exciting and absorbed every word Ásgeir said. It was a great experience to be there and talk to him, one thousand souls in the casual plane. I was surrounded by and filled with great calm while Ásgeir spoke, the anxiety and fear I had experienced when walking into Guðbjörg's apartment now completely gone. I felt comfortable there, and it all seemed so familiar, although I didn't know why.

"Well, it's time to say goodbye to you now," said Ásgeir. He added, "You're always welcome to come back to us. It is an honor to be with you. Goodbye."

There was a long silence, and finally Guðbjörg said with her own voice, "Hi." She smiled, reached for her glasses, and looked at us in turn. "That went well," she said with a smile.

"It was really great," I said.

"Are you satisfied with the meeting?" asked Guðbjörg.

"Very good," we both replied. We got up and walked to the coat rack in the lobby. I felt I wanted to stay there much longer. I felt like I had returned home after a long journey. I felt so calm and peaceful while listening to Ásgeir. I knew that outside, earthly conflict awaited me, accompanied by anxiety and fear. We said goodbye to Guðbjörg and thanked her and went down the stairs.

Once outside, I said, "This was remarkable and very interesting. What an experience."

My partner looked at me and said, "That was superb."

I sensed that something great and significant had happened in my life, but I didn't realize what it was exactly. I felt so good after the meeting, and for a long time afterward, I was very calm and peaceful. It was like embodying another existence that I didn't want to leave. Although Guðbjörg was a stranger to me, I felt a strong connection to her. I felt as if I had known her for a long time. "I'm going to come back here as soon as possible," I said, and my partner smiled.

The next day the phone rang, and I answered.

"Greetings." It was Guðbjörg. "Were you happy with the meeting yesterday?" she asked.

Spiritual Awakening

"Very," I replied. "It was a great experience. It was fun and exciting to talk to Ásgeir. I hope I can come back as soon as possible."

Guðbjörg replied, "You're always welcome." Then she added, "The magazine *Vikan* interviewed me and will publish the interview in the near future. They want to hear from a person who has done a session with me and ask them to describe how it felt and what the experience was like. Can I give them your name and number so they can call you and conduct a short interview?"

I felt it was a great honor to be able to help Guðbjörg and immediately replied, "Of course I'll do that."

"Thank you very much. They'll call you soon," said Guðbjörg. She added, "You are always welcome back for another session."

"Thank you very much. I would like that," I replied.

"Until next time," said Guðbjörg, and we said goodbye.

"This is a great honor," I thought to myself.

Soon afterward, a young woman called and introduced herself as a journalist for *Vikan*. She said she was working on an article about the medium Guðbjörg Sveinsdóttir and asked whether I had recently done a session with Guðbjörg and if she could ask me a few questions about my experience. It was all fresh in my memory, so it was easy for me to describe my experience. I told her that it was a remarkable and interesting meeting that had a great and positive effect on me. I had plenty of time to talk to

63

Guðbjörg before, and then the session was informative and positive in every way. I recommended that people went to Guðbjörg and said that I would definitely return to her as soon as possible. When I had explained my experience of the session, the journalist finally said, "This is great. I will use it along with the interview with Guðbjörg. May I accompany your story with '38-year-old male'?" I agreed, and she thanked me and said goodbye.

The turmoil in the financial markets had started to intensify, and many people talked about a complete economic collapse in Iceland if the government did not start taking action and reacting. During this time, I followed the news and politics in general. I favored the policy that individuals should have as much freedom as possible from the authorities—freedom in business and in one's own life. Then I thought, "If only my party got more MPs and more power, everything would be fine."

Those who predicted a collapse were seen as pessimistic and negative. Others spoke of it as a small storm that would pass quickly. The nation's rulers were still frequently abroad, and little was heard from them regarding the situation. All this talk of a crash had a negative effect on me, and this was a difficult time in my life.

Transformations and Collapse

About two weeks had passed since we were with Guðbjörg when I said, "I'm going to make another appointment with Guðbjörg. Would you like to join me?"

My partner looked at me. "Yes, I would. Count me in." It was nice to hear Guðbjörg's voice again when she answered the phone. We made an appointment and went to Guðbjörg to meet Ásgeir for a second time. Soon after I sat down on Guðbjörg's couch, I felt the same comfortable calm and inner peace as before. The monotony of everyday life was forgotten as I entered another world.

We talked with Guðbjörg before the meeting, and finally, she took off her glasses and put them on the table.

"Now something's happening," I said with a smile.

Guðbjörg smiled back, closed her eyes, and connected herself to Ásgeir. Finally, we heard his rough but gentle voice: "Well . . . Greetings to both of you, and welcome."

It seemed as though I had met an old and trusted friend again after a long absence. I felt tremendous security, became fearless, and enjoyed the comfort of sitting on the sofa. I forgot the time and place.

"What would you like to chat about today? And now, let's start with you, Viktor, if that's OK?" Ásgeir inquired.

I answered softly, "That's fine."

Ásgeir cleared his throat. "What would you like to talk about today?"

Like earlier, I took out the piece of paper with questions I had prepared. "I want to know the role of my mother."

There was silence, and then Ásgeir snapped his fingers and said, "Let's get her down here. Please go ahead." After a long pause, Ásgeir continued, "She's an artist and a priest like your wife and your friend here. What do you think about that?"

I thought for a while. "That fits her well."

Ásgeir said, "That's how it is. Do you have any further questions?"

I hadn't written the next question on the paper, but I popped it out without thinking: "What about my grandmother? What are her roles?"

Ásgeir was quick to answer: "Let's see . . . How old is she?"

I immediately replied, "She's seventy-eight years old."

As before, Ásgeir quickly found the roles that fit my grandmother well. "She's an artist and priest, same as your mother." I smiled, and Ásgeir added, "Look how you have arranged the priests around you. Isn't that remarkable?"

I looked at Ásgeir. "It's strange," I replied. "Are my mother and grandmother old souls like me?"

Ásgeir made a low and deep noise and then answered, "Yes, they are old souls but not as old as you. They are right behind you. They trail you closely." Then Ásgeir gently said, "Well, Viktor, can we turn to your friend?"

I replied gratefully, "Of course. Thank you very much."

"You're welcome. It's our pleasure speaking with you." Then Ásgeir turned to my partner and answered all his questions.

After that, the meeting was over, and Guðbjörg came back, opened her eyes, and put on her glasses. "Hi," she said quickly and looked at us alternately. "That went well," she added.

Now it was time to say goodbye and leave. Just like before, I didn't want to return to my everyday life. I felt so comfortable at Guðbjörg's place. We thanked Guðbjörg and said goodbye.

We had started to sense that economic conditions were deteriorating. The number of projects decreased and sales likewise. This caused me great distress. I became anxious and feared for our safety. However, we occasionally got some small projects that filled me with optimism again. My mood alternated up and down in this way. After a few weeks had passed since the last meeting with Guðbjörg, I felt a strong need and desire to meet her and Ásgeir again, so I made another appointment for us.

Ragnar Viktor Karlsson

We went to Guðbjörg, and I started talking to Ásgeir. All of a sudden, he said to me, "We want to ask you a favor."

I was curious and asked, "Sure, what is it?"

Ásgeir continued, "Since you're a good writer, we would like to ask you to write a book for us."

I felt this was a great honor and an interesting proposition. I moved around and adjusted myself on the couch, and without thinking about it, I answered, "Yes, I would like that. When should we begin?"

Ásgeir replied, "We'll let you know when it's convenient to start."

It was a great honor and very interesting to me because I had, for a long time, wanted to write a book for fun. This was also an interesting topic. We asked Ásgeir about our business and the hardships in the economy.

"You need to open your minds to new opportunities, get out of the office, and connect with others and even consider going abroad," answered Ásgeir.

I was greatly comforted at the meeting and felt an inner peace for several days. I started thinking about the book I would write for Ásgeir. "What's it supposed to be about?" I wanted to start right away. I thought a lot about the book over the next few weeks.

Finally, like many had predicted, a financial crisis hit. It spread like wildfire around the world. Many feared that the three Icelandic banks would go bankrupt, which would have unpredictable consequences for the Icelandic economy, companies, and households. People stepped forward, one after another, to defend the banks and say that there was no danger here in Iceland. Then the banks' lines of credit began closing one by one, and the first bank was bankrupt soon after. Then a little later, the other two fell. It was akin to a state of war, and there was great uncertainty about the security of the country. "Will we be able to buy fuel and food from abroad?" many people asked themselves.

Our phone stopped ringing, and business disappeared overnight. We completed the small projects we had and tried to collect the money we were owed. It didn't go well. It was as if all the money had disappeared from society overnight. The bills started piling up, and we could no longer pay for the upkeep of the building or our salaries. I was starting to feel like I was in a prison camp, and I couldn't move at all.

We went to work every day trying to figure out what we could do. I started looking for a job in Iceland, but there were few positions available. I applied for several but always received a negative response. My personal finances were getting bad, and I started receiving threatening letters from lawyers regarding small amounts. Our reserve fund was quickly depleted as I no longer had a salary. The situation affected me a lot. I was very anxious and fearful and had trouble sleeping. I often woke up in the middle of the night and lay awake until morning.

Ragnar Viktor Karlsson

All doors seemed closed in Iceland, and I had no desire to move abroad. I was happy in Iceland and felt that I was done with the chapter of my life where I lived abroad. Eventually, I started applying for jobs in Denmark, but there were few opportunities available. The economy was also tight in Denmark, although things were a bit better than in Iceland. Most of the replies I received from Denmark were negative. I got two interviews in a short time but was rejected in both.

Soon after we couldn't pay the mortgage on the commercial property, the bank started harassing us and demanding payment. A lot of people were passing through the shop at that time, and among them were tradesmen and others who were in trouble due to the crisis. There we heard that a lot of work was available in Norway for tradesmen and technicians. They needed people and had now started headhunting in Iceland. "I won't move to Norway," I said to my partner when the two of us sat at our desks. I neither wanted nor desired to move abroad.

Christmas was approaching, and we hadn't been paid in a long time. The situation was such that one person working could no longer support our families, so things were tight for both of us. "How are we supposed to celebrate Christmas with no money?" I asked one morning. My partner walked into our stockroom and started looking around. We found unopened parquet, some linoleum, and an expensive electric meter that we had bought but never used. We started collecting money by returning items and

70

being reimbursed. It worked, and we managed to pay ourselves a small salary just before Christmas 2008.

At the beginning of 2009, my partner and I decided to start looking for jobs in Norway. We began by searching online and discovered many jobs and recruitment agencies that helped us locate work opportunities. I prepared my CV and applications in Danish because I didn't know much Norwegian. We both immediately received a lot of feedback, and we started getting calls from Norway. Some people wanted to hire us right away. We went to Bergen together for an interview that yielded little despite the great need. Finally, an exciting and interesting job came with a company that designed and built machines for producing hydrogen from water. Then, in June, I was invited to an interview at the company, which was located in Notodden in southern Norway.

The interview went well, and when it was over, I asked the manager when I would get answers. "Within a few days," he replied with a smile. He said he would walk me to the bus that would take me to the airport so I could catch the flight to Iceland. While we were walking to the bus, he said to me, "We want to offer you the job, and we hope you will join us?"

I gave a big smile. "Yes, I want that. When can I start?" I wanted to start as soon as possible to begin receiving income again.

He replied, "It's best if you could start at the beginning of August. Then, everyone will be back from summer holidays and can help you get started on the job. You'll hear more from me next week."

I got on the bus and sat down. This was a great relief. Finally, I had a job and an income in sight.

We went for a last visit to Guðbjörg before I left for Norway. I asked Ásgeir if we should start the book he had talked about at the last meeting.

"Let's wait with the book," he answered.

This was a big disappointment to me. "They've changed their minds. They must have lost their respect for me," I thought to myself.

We said goodbye to Guðbjörg after the meeting.

I spent the summer preparing for my trip to Norway. This wasn't something I wanted to do, but I felt compelled to earn some income for my family. In my mind, this was just a temporary project. The crisis would be resolved quickly, and everything would be back to normal shortly. It was difficult to see that the company we were building was slipping from our fingers. It was also very difficult for me to say goodbye to my wife, relatives, and friends. I wasn't ready to leave Iceland.

I flew to Norway at the beginning of August 2009 and checked into Hotel Brattrein in Notodden. I paid a reasonable monthly rent for the room. I was given a small room on the top floor with its own bath and shower, and on the floor below, there was a shared kitchen and lounge for guests. The only things in the kitchen were a fridge and a water heater. When I lay down on the pillow the first night, I started thinking, "Where am I, and what have I gotten myself into?" My mind was at home in Iceland with my wife, relatives, and friends and our company. I felt tears start to roll down my cheeks. I felt defeated, and it was a big shock for me. I was filled with great sadness, anger, and disappointment.

I went to work the next day and was well received by my colleagues. The work was interesting and fun. It was about a fifteen-minute walk from the hotel to the workplace. After a few days, I had adapted to this new environment. I went for long walks after work and on weekends. My mind and thoughts wandered during these walks. I imagined that the collapse was an external attack on Iceland, and now Icelanders would all have to come together as one in solidarity to save the country and nation from these troubles. Politicians would now have to work together as one and forget their partisan policies and differences. They would have to find a way to save the people and the households and build society anew. But the reality was different: two to three families were evicted from their homes every day for many months at the request of banks and other credit institutions. It seemed that the authorities used all their time and energy to save banks and financial institutions just to let families burn, and thousands lost their homes.

Thinking about these things made me feel sad and sympathize with these people. I did not understand this behavior of the rulers and started to think that something wasn't right. It dawned on me that the authorities were not working for the people of the country but were servants of invisible financial forces. I decided there and then to write off politics and avoid the polling station more often. "These people are not working for my interests in any way," I realized. I felt a lot of anger and hatred when I thought about these matters, and I felt like a victim.

A few months after I went to Norway, my partner got a job in the oil sector working on rigs in the Norwegian city of Stavanger.

I started thinking about Guðbjörg and Ásgeir. "It would be nice to meet them now," I thought to myself during one of my walks. I began reflecting on the book and what it should be about. "It would be nice to write a book where spiritual issues are woven into a plot. In this way, it would be possible to bring spiritual knowledge to as many people as possible," I thought to myself. There, the basic idea of the first book that I later wrote, *Konungur án krúnu (King Without a Crown)*, began to form. I envisioned an older man teaching spirituality to a younger man. I didn't think about it any further at the time, but it did cross my mind on occasion.

Halldóra had begun to push for her to move to Norway, and we would live there, but I wanted to move back to Iceland as soon as possible or as soon as the crisis was over. But the crisis dragged on, and there was no solution in sight. After I had lived in Hotel Brattrein for about a year, Halldóra called me and said, "I have booked a flight to Norway on Monday. I am moving there!" We rented a small apartment on the ground floor of a house, where the owners lived upstairs.

The company I worked for was a subsidiary of Statoil in Norway, but it was announced at one of the staff meetings that Statoil intended to sell the company. I had been a freelancer the entire time I had been there, but my boss was working on hiring me permanently when this news came. Thus, I was never hired on a permanent basis. This was a disappointment to me, and I felt that my position there had become extremely precarious, so I started applying for jobs in Denmark. It was very slow, and most of my applications were rejected. But eventually I got a job in Copenhagen with a company that designed equipment for waste incinerators that used the energy for heating. My wife and I, therefore, moved to Amager in Copenhagen at the beginning of 2010.

Moving from Notodden to the big city was a tremendous change. I sensed quickly that there was a lot of tension between people at the new workplace, and it was a difficult atmosphere. I felt that there was a lack of management from the supervisors, and I saw that this company would not survive for long. In a few months, I decided to look for another job.

At the time, there was much imbalance and rootlessness in my life. Deep down, I longed for balance and stability, but what I was experiencing was far from that. I moved from one job to another, and we moved around a lot during this time.

Ragnar Viktor Karlsson

It was difficult to find jobs in Denmark, and I wanted to leave the company I was working for in Copenhagen as soon as possible. I looked at the job ads in Denmark, and there wasn't much to choose from, so I started looking at what was available in Norway. One of the first things I saw was an ad that was clearly from my old company that had changed its name and moved from Notodden to Sandefjord in southern Norway. The ad had my former boss listed as a contact for the job. I got in touch and was subsequently hired as head of the electrical department, and we moved from Copenhagen to Sandefjord in Norway in the fall of 2010. Our stay in Denmark was short, lasting only nine months.

In my new job, I had the opportunity to travel around the world, which I really enjoyed. I appreciated meeting people with varying backgrounds from different cultures. The most memorable trips were the ones I made to Pune, India. I took five trips alone there and stayed for a week to ten days each time.

It was a foreign culture and fascinating. Everywhere you went and everywhere you looked, there were crowds of people. Every morning, I was picked up by a driver who took me to the factory where we were testing equipment that my company in Norway was buying. I worked until dinner, and then the driver came and took me back to the hotel. It was about a half-hour drive, and I observed the people on the way. In many places, I saw small shelters that people had put together with poles driven into the ground. Then, corrugated iron plates were laid onto the poles and served as outer walls. Finally, two plates were laid on top as a roof. Outside one small shelter stood a family consisting of a couple and two or three children. Near the shelter was a large tub with rainwater, where people were cleaning and bathing. In many parts of the city, there were garbage dumps that were on fire, and many people were rummaging through them in search of something valuable or food to eat. I started feeling sorry for these people and was filled with sympathy. One of the Indian engineers who I often worked with was always smiling, and he radiated joy and happiness. Once I walked up to him and said, "You smile."

"Of course," he replied. "Life is so wonderful, and I am so blessed."

I became curious. "Tell me about it."

He smiled even more. "I have just recovered from a major operation I had, and it was successful, and I am now healthy and sound. Then my family just bought a two-room apartment of about forty square meters, and now we have our own toilet and shower."

This I found interesting. "Are there many of you who live there?"

He replied with a smile, "No, there are eight of us."

I started thinking, "Forty square meters and eight people."

He continued, "Then I had the opportunity to educate myself, and I have a good job. I am so grateful for everything I have been given in life."

This conversation had a great impact on me and taught me a lot. I learned to be grateful for what I have and what I get. Nothing is guaranteed in life, not health, shelter, food, or clothing. After this conversation and what I had seen and experienced in India, I never again complained about my situation and what I had. It's about being happy and grateful for what you have instead of being unhappy about what you don't have. Within just a few minutes, this happy man had opened my eyes to what happiness is and what it is not.

These trips to India were a valuable experience for me and had a profound effect on my views and expectations of life. While there, I realized that happiness in life is not based on wealth and worldly goods but instead comes from within and depends on a person's state of mind.

My business partner from Iceland had not found the job he was seeking in Stavanger, so it wasn't long before he and I started working together in Sandefjord. There was plenty to do and many projects, and he liked the tasks that we gave him. We started going for walks in the neighborhood during our lunch breaks and soon began reminiscing about the good times we had at our company in Iceland. Then we started discussing whether we should continue with the company where we left off. We thought of negotiating with our bosses at Nel Hydrogen to subcontract our company in Iceland. That way, we could raise money to get the company up and running again. I was hesitant about this in the beginning, as I was comfortable at Nel Hydrogen. The projects were exciting, and there was a positive atmosphere among the employees.

While we were considering these matters, the rumor spread that Nel Hydrogen was not doing well and that its future was uncertain. "Here we go again," I thought to myself. Then I received an email from the bosses indicating that everyone had to work together to save money in the company. As soon as I received this email, I realized that the ship was leaking and that it was only a matter of time before it went down. Most of my colleagues took it lightly and said it wasn't serious. One girl who was a good friend and colleague seemed to understand the gravity of the situation and asked me, "What should we do now, Viktor?"

I gave her a serious look and answered, "Update your CV."

My partner and I, therefore, decided to move forward with our idea of becoming subcontractors and trying to remain as such for as long as possible. We resigned from our positions, became subcontractors, and continued our work through our company in Iceland. But it didn't last long because a few months later, Nel Hydrogen was bankrupt, and our work there came to an end. However, some time later, new investors arrived and rebuilt the company. Since then, it has become a large international company with many employees, although I did not participate in that chapter since it occurred after my departure.

Ragnar Viktor Karlsson

Now that the work at Nel Hydrogen was done, we decided to move back to Iceland and establish our company there. In 2013, we moved to Iceland. While we lived in Norway, we had sold our house in Álftanes and bought an apartment, which is where we moved when we returned to Iceland. Our company leased a commercial space in Reykjavík, where we planned to start a lighting shop and electrical design office, just like before. We had begun again and were going to pick up where we left off.

Soon after we got home, I said to my partner, "I'm going to see if I can get an appointment with Guðbjörg."

My partner liked the idea and said, "Make an appointment for both of us."

I was eager to meet Guðbjörg after a long absence and have the opportunity to speak with Ásgeir. Guðbjörg welcomed us joyfully. Before connecting with Ásgeir, Guðbjörg stared at me for a long time and then said, "It's not often that I see this color of aura here on the sofa. This beautiful orange is the color of kings."

I looked at Guðbjörg in surprise. "This is proof that she is connected to those above. No one could have remembered this," I thought to myself.

We talked to Ásgeir, who liked the idea of us starting our company in Iceland. Therefore, we received some support for our idea. However, the projects that we had expected in Iceland didn't materialize. The economy wasn't as far along as we had anticipated. We were remodeling the store, and the money we had saved ran out quickly. So, we sat down and looked for ways to generate more income for the company. We explored the idea of being hired as subcontractors in Norway, as we had planned to do at Nel Hydrogen, and use that opportunity as a springboard to get started in the Icelandic market. Halldóra and I were both ready to go back to Norway, so I suggested the possibility of us staying there for a year and receiving income from the new location. It would be easier for us to move to Norway temporarily as my partner had small children of preschool age.

So I started looking for work in Norway and, within a few weeks, found a job in Asker in the south of Norway. Halldóra and I moved back to Norway after a few months in Iceland.

Spiritual Awakening

We rented an apartment in Asker with everything we needed and moved there in September 2013. There was no public transportation in the neighborhood where we lived, and the nearest store was about twenty minutes by foot from our home. It took me about forty-five minutes to walk to work. I enjoyed walking, however, so this suited me well. The job was exciting and interesting, and it was a good place to work, with fine people.

It was during my walks to and from work that my spiritual awakening began. I started to wonder how so many things seemed to be going in the wrong direction in the world. I had believed that the authorities and politicians were doing their best to improve people's lives and living conditions. Taxes and fees seemed to rise steadily, while public services seemed to decrease at the same time. I started thinking about the municipalities. Local taxes had reached their highest level, and real estate taxes increased at the end of each year. Then a garbage fee was added, and simultaneously, the frequency of waste collection was reduced. Then there was the drainage fee and the water fee, and the list went on and on. Despite more income and fewer services, the City of Reykjavík only accumulated debt.

"This cannot be a normal development. Something about this doesn't add up," I thought to myself. With all the technological advances that had happened in the last few years, things should have been improving. Likewise, taxes and fees should have been decreasing and services increasing. If the services were improved, new fees were added as well. It was the same at the government level: taxes and fees increased while services were reduced. People had to pay more and more for the services they received from the public sector.

The health-care system was a good example of this. Most of the hospitals were understaffed, and people were no longer able to recover in the hospital after having an operation. The queues to have an operation and receive services also kept getting longer. In the past, people received treatment and care after having operations and were allowed to recover in the hospital, but now people were sent home while very sick immediately after an operation. Despite the high taxes, people had to pay increasingly high fees for all services in the health-care system. It was also becoming difficult for the elderly to enter old age and nursing homes, despite having paid taxes to the state all their lives.

I was filled with anger at all these thoughts. All this was a deterioration and not normal. "What's the cause?" I thought to myself. Taxes and fees for car owners were rising steadily, and the roads were getting worse as maintenance was decreased. The state had never received so much income from car owners, and at the same time, the authorities complained that they didn't have the funds to maintain and improve the road system. They even talked about imposing road tolls to cover the costs.

"How much tax is levied on one loaf of bread?" I thought to myself. The farmer who grows the wheat pays taxes on the land, and taxes are also included in the price of the machines that he purchases. When he pays himself a salary, he pays taxes. All these taxes are added to the price of the commodity. Then the person who transports the grain to the baker pays fees and taxes on the car, on the fuel, and then on his wages. This is also added to the price of bread. Then the baker pays taxes on his housing as well as his salary. This, as well as the VAT, is added to the selling price. Taxes and fees have been piled on the price of bread, all the way from the farmer to the consumer.

"These are hidden taxes," I thought to myself.

I started thinking about what my profession of engineering was like forty to fifty years ago, before the era of computers. Back then, everything had to be drawn by hand, and all text was typed on typewriters. There were no computers or emails, and all designs took much longer. Today, all communication is faster, and everything can be drawn and processed on a computer, so things are much less time consuming. Why aren't the working hours shortened by an equivalent amount? Or the salary increased? Where did the difference go? Was it stolen? The same was true of many other professions.

The benefits of technological advances did not find their way to the people in the form of a shorter work week or better working conditions. The middle class was steadily being wiped out over the years. If you look way back in time, the middle class had servants in their homes, and the husband worked while the wife took care of the home and children. Today, in most cases, both the husband and wife are required to work outside the home, and living conditions are steadily deteriorating.

In my mind, I reviewed many aspects of society in a critical light. "This is not a natural development," I thought to myself.

When the politician steps forward and speaks, especially before the elections, he says, "Living conditions have never been as good, and we have never invested as much money in health care and services for the elderly."

But my experience was different.

I started thinking about my experience with the economic crash and how the politicians went against the people and sided with the banks and financial companies. "What the bank doesn't steal from me, the government takes," I thought to myself. A great rage arose within me at all these thoughts. People's standard of living and livelihoods are based upon decisions made by the authorities—decisions made by a handful of people. Surveillance of human activities seemed to be increasing steadily, and individual freedom was decreasing accordingly. Little can be done without permission from the government.

Spiritual Awakening

"Every war in the world is a result of decisions made by politicians," I thought to myself. All my thoughts and everything I had been pondering were focused on the political class and the authorities. These things weren't laws of nature, and it would be easy to reverse the current trend in favor of the people and society. "Why is it like this?" I questioned. "What drives people to tear down and steal? I have never agreed or consented to paying all these taxes. The authorities reach into my pockets and take from me without permission. Taking something without permission is called stealing."

It reminded me of when I was supposed to vote for parliament for the first time, and I went to my grandmother and asked her, "What should I vote for, Grandma?"

Grandma looked at me and quickly answered, "I'll just vote for my Savior. He'll never betray me."

It was a strange answer that I didn't understand at the time, but on my walks to work in Norway, I began to understand what my grandmother had meant. Now I completely agreed with her.

In previous years, I enjoyed politics and followed them closely. Then people discussed right- and left-wing policies, red and blue, etc. I watched and listened to many television and radio programs where "the big issues" were dissected to the core. There, the leaders appeared over and over again and were proud of their work, boasting about how well they succeeded in improving people's lives and living conditions and that never before had as much money been spent on this or the other issue. But when I was walking to and from work and I started to think about how things have developed in recent years, I sensed that everything was going downhill. I realized that all these TV and radio programs contained mere words to keep people hopeful.

I thought of the farmers, but on my travels around the country, I saw one farm after another be abandoned and old machines rusting outside. "When the farms are too small, farming isn't sustainable." This was the policy of the authorities. "How can it not be sustainable to produce food when people go hungry in many parts of the world?" I considered. Humans are one big family and should stick together.

Winter was coming to Asker, Norway, and I was sometimes cold going to work when there was frost and it was about fifteen degrees with no wind at all. The snow crunched under my shoes with every step. I kept thinking about these things when I walked to and from work. The politicians' actions can actually be broken down into three categories, I realized. They keep us down financially and make sure we don't do too well so that we stay stuck in the rat race. They do this with taxes and fees. They steadily reduce our human rights and freedoms through legislation and stricter regulations. Our common natural resources are then placed in the hands of a select few.

"We are steadily being constrained more and more," I thought to myself during a cold winter morning when the weather was clear and the moon cast a bluish light on the snow. "Why does it seem like the rulers actually work against the people instead of working with them? Are the rulers bribed or threatened?" I wondered as I struggled to understand. If you don't understand something, it's because you lack information.

It was the same in Norway and in Denmark, where the rulers seemed to follow the same script. The Danish welfare system, which was exemplary during my student years in Aalborg, had deteriorated for the people of the country. Those on benefits and who had the lowest wages found it increasingly difficult to make ends meet, and rules and regulations became ever more complex. This wasn't a natural development; there must have been responsible forces that controlled the situation from behind the scenes, forces that we the people of the country did not know about and did not see.

These thoughts consumed me during my walks and didn't have a positive effect on me. I was filled with anger and even hatred. I began to perceive myself as a prisoner in a slave camp. I had to work whether I like it or not, just to be able to afford shelter, food, and clothing. It was an unpleasant feeling, as if I were a prisoner of a system that made sure I didn't escape to freedom. "They steal everything from me," I thought to myself. "How can I escape this system that controls every aspect of our lives? I would need to move away to the countryside and do subsistence farming in order to disconnect from this system that does nothing but steal my property without giving me anything in return." Anger began to rise within me when I had these thoughts. "Even if we moved into a small hut in the countryside, we would have to pay property taxes on the hut and the plot, so we would always have to have an income. There is no escaping this," I concluded. "I am an unfree prisoner and a slave to this system," I thought.

These reflections dragged me down and made me sad. Instead of ceasing my thoughts on the matter, I continued. It went on like this for a while.

My partner was at home in Iceland and was preparing the lighting shop and getting the company up and running. I liked my job. The projects were exciting, and there was good morale. There were people from many nationalities, and I enjoyed talking to and getting to know the individuals from different cultures. There were many Indians, and I worked with them a lot.

Once when I was sitting in the canteen eating lunch at the same table as people from India, Norway, Sweden, and Iran, the thought came to me that if the economic collapse had not happened in Iceland, I would never have had the chance to experience this, getting to know different people from a variety of backgrounds and traveling around the world experiencing a wide range of countries and cultures. It was a great experience for me.

Halldóra often met me when I walked home from work, and we would walk home together. The days were short during the winter, and now I walked to and from work in the dark. It was good to have Halldóra meet me because then we could chat on the way home. We sometimes went to Oslo on weekends and took the train there. It was nice to take a day off and walk around the city.

These thoughts of mine about the authorities and politics continued for several weeks. I obsessed about this over and over, but then one morning while I was walking to work, my perception began to change and open up. I had a vision: a small group of people had, for a long time, been at the helm behind the scenes. A group that few know exists, let alone know is in charge. I saw how the group increasingly took control of the authorities in different countries, ruling each one separately through the local politicians. I had never experienced such strong visions and sensations before.

I saw the goals of the group and the kind of future it wanted to build for humanity. I saw members of the group sitting in red plush chairs with high backs at a huge round table. It was all so real. The group planned to form a one-world government and destroy democracy. I saw how it had taken control of most of the media and determined what people heard and saw. What people got to see on the news was either a hoax or only part of the truth. Few people knew that this group existed because it was never talked about in the mainstream media. I saw how it had planned and started most wars in the past.

I started to experience a great fear within me. The strategy was to turn all the world's inhabitants into destitute slaves, with the "authorities" monitoring every move and action that individuals make. The group wanted control over energy, water, and food. It controlled education and kept important information and knowledge from the masses. All these changes were made in small incremental steps so that people would pay little attention to them and have no idea what is going on. The group controlled the monetary system, and the strategy was to steal as much as possible from the public. Money is a tool used to keep people enslaved. It provided all the entertainment for the people to keep them busy and distracted from what was really happening. I sensed that the group was interested in reducing the human race. Stealing, killing, and destroying were the only goals these people had. I saw and experienced how a few people could cause great distress and death to many, and it was all willfully planned.

When I approached the workplace, it was as if I was waking up and coming back into this world. I had no recollection of walking to work that morning. These visions overwhelmed my senses. I was amazed at what had happened and how much information I had received in such a short time. I started to wonder about it all. "What the hell happened?" I asked myself as I walked through the door of the workplace. I felt in my heart that all this was correct. The sensation was so strong and real. I never doubted what I saw and sensed there. I had seen the whole picture. My eyes had been opened to the truth of what was happening in the world. When I compared this to my speculations about politics and the actions of politicians, it all started to come together. I finally began to understand the actions of the politicians.

Spiritual Awakening

My experience that morning had a profound and lasting effect on me. I experienced this as a big shock. I had believed that everything in the world happened by a series of coincidences and not that things were controlled by a small group of people who had evil intentions.

This was a huge surprise to me. Everything I had believed and the world in which I lived were one big illusion, a performance where the script was written by evil and malicious people. I felt that I was entering a grieving process. I began to experience a deep sadness in my heart and felt great compassion for humanity.

The next morning, the visions continued to come to me. I saw great suffering for many, famine, war, and homeless people. People looking for food and water. I saw a lot of sick people who had nowhere to lay their heads and received no help. I saw death and disaster everywhere.

I began to feel all these sufferings inside me. I felt a stab in the chest and started to feel sick. I experienced the suffering of humanity in my heart, which was full of sorrow. It was a striking experience that was so strong and real. I started to lose my appetite and entered a deep depression that lasted for a long time. This had such a profound effect on me that my wife asked if something was wrong. I didn't know what to say, but I decided to tell her about my experience and informed her what I had sensed a few days before. When I finished telling her about this, she replied, "I feel like I've always known this. We just need to stand together and take care of each other." I accepted that because I sensed that there would be great conflict on Earth in the coming years.

I had a hard time concentrating on work for the next few weeks, and my heart was constantly full of sadness. "Am I the only one who has sensed such things?" I wondered to myself one morning on my way to work. "Who should I talk to?" I started to feel very lonely and isolated. These perceptions and my desire to open up occurred during the winter of 2013 to 2014. At this point, I had no idea what was happening and where this would lead me.

I started searching the internet to see if there was anyone out there who had experienced something similar to what I had sensed. Then I found a lot of videos where people were talking about the shadow power and their actions and plans, and much of what I saw fit what I had experienced. "Strange," I thought to myself. "I'm not the only one." I started looking at a lot of material, and it mostly fit my visions and perceptions. There was a great conflict between good and evil occurring in the world. A conflict that few knew was taking place.

One of the things I encountered on the internet was people talking about the Bilderberg Meetings, which are annual meetings that started in 1954. The first one was held in a Dutch hotel called the Bilderberg. The meeting has since been held in many parts of the world. The world's political leaders, CEOs of large companies, and rich and influential people congregate there and hold private meetings for several days. What I found peculiar about this was that I had never heard these meetings mentioned in any news media. "It must be newsworthy that so many influential people meet," I thought to myself. This underlined that my perception was correct, namely, that these people manage and control the media and what's covered and what isn't. At this moment, I decided never to believe any news coverage from the mainstream media.

The period after my visions and opening up was difficult for me. My heart was full of sadness, and I felt great compassion for humanity. I also experienced a lot of anger and hatred toward those in control. I started reviewing much content online over the next few months, where people from all over the world were discussing these things from various angles. Often these videos created a lot of fear, and many of them claimed that the world would end shortly. Nowhere did I see any suggestions for a solution that would free humanity from this shadow power that hung over us like a black cloud.

I began to follow the news and what the politicians were doing and quickly saw that it all matched the visions I had. The main theme of legislation was increasing taxes and the cost of services and curtailing human rights and freedom. The media employed lies and deception so that most people welcomed the loss of freedom. I found this very sad to watch. The authorities deceived people with the help of the media in order to achieve their goals.

Many people were in a bad place financially. Many were feeling ill mentally but did not realize what the cause was.

I quickly discovered that it was not easy to point out to people what was happening. Many seemed blind to the truth and believed in the system and the authorities and that they were doing everything they could to protect us and improve our living conditions. When I explained to people what was happening, it fell on deaf ears. "Don't you need to take some time off? Haven't you been working too much lately?" I once heard when I was speaking about what was really going on in the world. In the following months, I began to think about how to ease the suffering of other people, to open their eyes to what was happening and improve their mental and physical well-being.

My wife Halldóra and I had been in Asker for over a year, and we both felt good. However, one day I felt that I wanted to move back to Iceland. This desire became stronger and stronger, and I started pressuring Halldóra to come to Iceland, but she did not want to go back. Then we decided to return to Iceland. I went to my boss in Asker and told him that we were going to move to Iceland, but I was very interested in continuing to work for them in some way. He suggested that I work remotely from Iceland but that I would have to come to Norway for one week each month. I agreed to this, and we went back to Iceland in the spring of 2015.

I started doing the Norwegian job at the office of our company and then went to Norway once a month as agreed, and I stayed there for one week at a time.

Spiritual Opening

My wife Halldóra had not gone to Guðbjörg. Halldóra wasn't ready to come with me when I went to see Guðbjörg a few years before. But one day Halldóra said to me, "Should we go to Guðbjörg together?" She didn't have to ask me twice, and I made an appointment for us. It was nice to see Guðbjörg again after such a long time. A lot had happened in my life since the last time I saw her. Guðbjörg connected to Ásgeir, who confirmed Halldóra's soul roles, which were artist and priest.

When it was my turn to talk to Ásgeir, I told him what I had perceived about the world and the ruling powers. Finally I asked, "Is my perception correct? Is it really this way?"

Ásgeir replied, "Yes, you are right, my dear friend."

We then wrapped up the meeting and said our thanks.

I still wondered about how I could help people feel better and end their suffering. I felt a strong desire to help others, but I didn't know how to do it. I had made up my mind to move away from the city to the countryside to enjoy the quiet and escape from the hustle and bustle of city life. "Living in the countryside and writing books would suit me well," I thought to myself. Ideally, I wanted to live in a cabin deep in the woods or on a mountain where I could be alone and secluded from all people and distractions. I started to think about the book I would write. "It would be good to start it now," I decided. I felt a desire to teach. I just didn't know what I wanted to teach. I grew more and more fascinated with becoming a teacher and writing books and living outside the city.

I felt a contradiction within me. I had developed a strong calling and desire to help people, but at the same time, I wanted to withdraw as much as possible away from people and all distractions and to move to a secluded place. I realized that my feelings were opposites that did not go together.

One morning while Halldóra and I were having breakfast, I said to her, "Wouldn't it be nice to move to the country, away from the hustle and bustle of the city, and enjoy being in nature and listening to the birds in the spring and summer?"

Halldóra smiled and answered right away, without hesitation, "Yes, that would be great. I don't enjoy the city anymore." Halldóra liked the countryside as she was born and raised there.

"I can realize my dream of writing books and even start teaching," I explained. Both of us thought these ideas were very interesting. "How about opening a spiritual center with the purpose of helping people feel better? We could welcome people who could stay for a few days and get away from the stress of everyday life and get in touch with nature and themselves. I can teach what I have already learned and write books in the meantime." I was on a roll with these ideas and was already there in my mind.

Halldóra thought my ideas were very interesting and exciting. At that time, we lived in an apartment at Krummahólar 8 in Breiðholt. Almost every day, I went to the hot tub at the swimming pool in Breiðholt, where I felt the fatigue and tension disappear from my body. It was there that I started planning our spiritual school. "I will kill many birds with one stone," I thought to myself. I'll be in the countryside, teach, and write books, and make a difference. That was all I wanted to do. My mind had started to drift away from our company and its operation, but I still worked remotely through the internet for the Norwegian company in Asker and mostly stayed in Iceland.

Halldóra and I decided to make another appointment with Guðbjörg at the end of July 2015. When Guðbjörg had established a connection with Ásgeir, he started talking to Halldóra.

Afterward, Ásgeir said to me, "Well, Viktor, what would you like to talk about today?"

I quickly replied, "I feel like I'm experiencing a spiritual awakening and great changes are brewing within me. Now I feel that the TV, movies, music, news, and being around other people is a distraction, and I prefer to be alone."

Ásgeir cleared his throat. "You're starting to open up, my friend. When that happens, you become sensitive and don't tolerate distractions well. It also takes very little to disturb your peace. People engage in more small talk. That is to say, they don't engage in it more, but rather, you begin to notice better. You become absent-minded and can't follow along and simply can't participate in it. You might act a bit silly and not know what to do with yourself while the person talks on and on."

"I have experienced this," I agreed.

Ásgeir continued, "You desire to talk about the true state of the world, but there is no one around you who takes an interest in those matters. This causes you to feel lonely. Yours is a lonely journey, but while you're opening up, it's best to avoid all distractions for the time being. During this spiritual awakening, your group of friends will be shuffled. You'll no longer get along with some of the people you've known for years. The friendships will end by themselves. The deeper you delve into spiritual matters, the stronger you become, and eventually, there will be little that can disturb your peace. Your understanding of people will deepen, and then you will start to develop tolerance. Your thinking will also become clearer."

I listened carefully to what Ásgeir said. "Yes, I'm starting to have a better perspective on life and my existence, and I feel like I have a greater and deeper understanding of things," I answered.

Ásgeir continued, "It's difficult and lonely to change like you are doing now. Few people go through this, and it is easy to give up. It would be preferable if more people did this."

I added, "I feel very rootless right now. I can't see very far into the future, and I feel a lot of instability."

There was a short silence, and then Ásgeir continued, "It's because you're losing interest in the job you're doing."

"Yes, my job doesn't give me pleasure like it used to," I confessed. "Halldóra and I would like to move to the countryside and start a spiritual school or center to help people feel better and develop a deeper connection with themselves. We just don't know where and how to do it."

Guðbjörg began to smile broadly, and Ásgeir said, "We like listening to you now, friend." He continued, "We like this idea and will support you along the way. It might be situated right here just outside the city so that the city dwellers don't have to drive far to visit you. Then you should have them help you with the housework and preparing the food and tidying up. Teaching people to work together is a big part of spiritual teaching."

I was very excited and couldn't wait to get started on this idea. "Although I can't channel information to people, I could take care of the administrative side and teach people what I have learned from you." In my mind, channeling like Guðbjörg did was an innate talent that very few possessed.

"There are many people who can channel and can help you," answered Ásgeir.

"Finally, I've found a way to help people feel better. This is what I was looking for when I was opening up in

Norway," I thought to myself. "I can write spiritual books as well and help people that way," I added.

"How about you start the first book now and finish it before Christmas? You should make a firm decision, and it's best that you find a fixed time of day to write. Then it will go quickly and smoothly," Ásgeir said.

"I like this. I'll do it this way and get started right away," I replied with a smile.

After a long silence, Ásgeir asked, "Have you ever wanted to go to Tibet?"

I immediately answered, "Yes, I have often thought about it."

Ásgeir asked Halldóra as well. "What about you?"

Halldóra answered affirmatively: "Yes, it would be nice to go there."

"Would you not go there with him?" Ásgeir added. "You would enjoy seeing the monks and talking to them."

I smiled. "Can you talk to the monks?"

Ásgeir said, "We think so. You are connected to them. There are many of them right here, right now, all around you. So we think you should go to Tibet and see it all. It's like coming home when you get there. You have lived many lives there in Tibet, and Halldóra has been there two or three times."

I was excited about the prospect and asked, "Were we together in Tibet?"

Ásgeir replied, "Yes, you were both men and great friends. You were both monks."

After a long silence, Ásgeir said, "While we've been chatting, your spiritual guides have been sending energy to you and working with your body, my friend. They are helping you to open up, and you will feel changes in the next few days."

"I'm thankful for that," I replied. "Thank you for the help."

Finally, Ásgeir said, "Allow your idea of the spiritual school to take shape within you, and let it develop." Then Ásgeir ended the meeting. "Best of luck, friends—in all respects, my dear friends. Don't be afraid; everything has its own way. Thank you."

I thought long and hard about this meeting with Ásgeir and Guðbjörg. One could say that it was a groundbreaking meeting that marked the beginning of my spiritual journey and career.

After this meeting at the end of July 2015, my life was going to change completely, and I had no idea what the future would bring to me.

Internal Conflict and Struggle

I had developed a great interest in spiritual matters, which increased day by day. At this time, I was mostly interested in gaining as much knowledge and wisdom as possible about these issues. I now looked on the internet for material about spiritual matters instead of reading about the state of the world and what the shadow powers were doing. A world that wasn't there a few weeks earlier was opening up to me. I quickly found a lot of material online that I started reviewing, but I mostly looked at videos in which spiritual teachers and "masters" taught and guided their disciples. I immersed myself in these topics and always wanted to know more.

I started my first book, *Konungur án Krúnu* (*King without a Crown*), and followed Ásgeir's advice to set aside a fixed time every day to write. On weekdays I wrote from six to eight at night, and on weekends from nine in the morning to one in the afternoon. I stuck to this schedule, and the writing went well. As before, I was working for the Norwegian company in Asker, so I went to Norway one week each month and stayed at the Scandic Hotel in Asker. I stuck to my writing schedule and wrote in the hotel room.

Now that I had finally started writing, and I enjoyed it. Writing books felt very fulfilling to me. When I was in Iceland, I either went to the hot tub at the swimming pool in Breiðholt after work or for a nice walk around Elliðaárdalur. This way, I managed to relieve the tension in my body and clear my mind after work so that I was ready to sit down to write. At the time, it was very difficult for me to clear my mind, as it was constantly all over the place. I had begun to map out our spiritual center in my mind and wondered how it would turn out. I thought about the writing and about publishing the book. I thought a lot about the meeting with Guðbjörg and Ásgeir and everything that happened there. This was a big turning point in my life, and I had much to think about.

I knew that my time at our company was over, and my way of thinking was incompatible with my business partner and the projects we did there. My interest in the business was gone, and I felt within myself that we were parting ways. My focus had shifted, and now the spiritual matters occupied my whole mind.

I had developed a strong calling to help people and to make a difference. My spiritual journey had begun. Deep down, I sensed that this was the only true way.

The scenes of people's suffering and discomfort that I had pictured so vividly some time ago had now become my driving force to do good. They had started me on this journey that had begun.

Two days after meeting with Guðbjörg, I woke up at home and felt a bit strange. I couldn't quite place it, but something wasn't right. My wife continued sleeping when I got up, so I got dressed and went to the bathroom. When I looked in the bathroom mirror, I saw how swollen my face was. My cheeks were inflamed, and my eyes were sunken. I pushed on my cheeks, but I didn't feel anything. Yet I felt like I had slept for a week. I felt rested and comfortable. I went to Halldóra's bedside to say goodbye before I went down to the shop for work. I told her how I felt but that I was going to work.

"Just come back home if you get sick," she said.

I agreed and drove off to work. It had been decided that I would be alone in the shop that day. I sat down at my desk and had barely started working when I felt love and well-being wash over me. It happened quickly, and soon I felt infinite love in my heart and ecstasy in every cell of my body. All my anxiety, pain, and fear were gone. An indescribable euphoria flowed through me, and I wanted to embrace everything and everyone due to the love I experienced. I sensed that I feared nothing, and I was completely carefree and fearless. "This is remarkable. I've always wanted to feel this way," I thought to myself as I sat alone at the desk in the shop. "My spiritual guides on the other side are helping me. This is proof of it." This strengthened my faith in spiritual matters and removed the tiny doubt I had. I could see everything around me so clearly, and all the colors had become deeper and stronger. My mind was clear and very calm. I enjoyed every moment and found it difficult to concentrate on work.

The day passed in bliss, and I went home. I decided to go for a nice walk, so I went down to Elliðaárdalur and walked around in the forest. It was wonderful to see how strong and deep the colors were. I had never seen the colors of nature and the environment so strong and beautiful. It was a pleasure to walk there among the trees. The birds' singing had never been so beautiful. I felt as if the sparrows were coming closer than before and followed me to cheer me up with their singing. Suddenly I felt like I was in paradise. "In an instant, everything has changed, including my perception and experience," I realized. "Such bliss I get to experience." After the walk, I went home to write, and the text flowed smoothly. Writing had never been so easy and comfortable.

Two days later I had to go to Norway because of my work, and I took Halldóra with me. The sense of well-being and ecstasy remained in my body and had not faded at all. "I will always feel this way" is what I thought on our way to Norway. I felt this way day and night for a week, but on the seventh day, I sensed that the feeling and well-being began to fade away slowly. This was a big disappointment because now I started to feel as I had before. I felt the knot of anxiety in my stomach and the worries start to surface, and everything seemed to be going the same way as before. "This is terrible," I thought. "Why did I have to lose it?" This was followed by great distress and disappointment for many days.

Halldóra and I went back home to Iceland, and I maintained my daily routine and continued writing as before. During my walks, I started thinking, "If I could feel like this for a week, I must be able to feel like this again. I need to figure out how to do that." I felt hopeful. "Maybe spirituality is about feeling this way all the time, every day and every night. That's why spiritual masters sit for hours in meditation in the lotus position with their eyes closed." I was now fully focused on finding this ecstasy again. That unconditional love in my heart that pushed the anxiety, fear, and worry out of my life for good. Spirituality was changing from a search for knowledge and information to a search for well-being and ecstasy. "I need to achieve this feeling again," I thought to myself.

But what did not disappear was this deep perception of nature and wildlife around me and all these deep and strong colors that had now appeared to me.

My walks around Elliðaárdalur had become longer, and I mostly walked along the narrow paths in the forests. There I could be by myself, and I enjoyed seeing the colors of nature and smelling the vegetation and trees. The birds sang beautiful songs to me. This experience had never been so strong before. That's why I strove to spend more and more time outside in nature. After a long walk, I went home and continued writing the book.

Two weeks after we were with Guðbjörg, I wanted to see her again to go over what I had experienced and talk more about the spiritual school we wanted to establish. I called her around the middle of August to make an appointment, but she said she was sick and would call me when she was better. I waited anxiously to hear from Guðbjörg as the days passed.

On the last Saturday of August, Halldóra and I decided to go berry picking and drove up to Hvalfjörður in beautiful weather and went into Brynjudalur. We were picking berries when my phone rang. I saw it was Guðbjörg.

"Good to hear from you," I said.

"I'm brewing myself some coffee. Do you know what that means?" Guðbjörg asked.

"Can I come now?" I asked with great anticipation.

"Yes, we want to have you over as soon as possible. Can you come tonight?"

I stood up. "Yes, I can make it tonight," I replied without thinking.

"Come around eight. I'm looking forward to seeing you. Bye."

I said goodbye and was filled with anticipation. I told Halldóra about the conversation, and she was happy for me. We continued picking berries into the afternoon and then drove home. After dinner, I drove off to Guðbjörg in Hlíðarhjalli in Kópavogur. My heart was racing as I walked into the lobby of the apartment building and rang the doorbell. There was static on the intercom, and then I heard Guðbjörg say, "Come on in, Viktor."

I went up the stairs. "A lot has changed since I first walked up those stairs," I thought to myself.

Guðbjörg was standing in the doorway on the top floor when I came up. She welcomed me and offered me coffee, and then we sat down in the living room. "There are multiple people who want to talk to you tonight. They appeared here as soon as you walked in. They want to connect directly with me, and I was immediately overshadowed, even though I haven't let them in yet."

As soon as we finished the coffee, Guðbjörg began connecting. "Hello, dear friend" was the first thing she said when the people had connected. They continued, "It's an honor to have you with us. We have waited for you for a long time. It was always known that you would go down this path and work with us. You will write books and hold lectures to help people. We need a person like you who can write and has the roles that you do. We have plenty of material to write about, and there can be many books if you are ready."

I looked at Guðbjörg, stunned. "I'm ready," I answered quickly.

I then related what I had experienced a few weeks earlier when my body was filled with ecstasy and I became fearless and carefree for a week.

"We are opening you up, friend, as a writer and speaker. This was the first step in opening you and your body to our energy," they explained.

I tensed up. "Will I experience this again?"

They quickly replied, "Yes, you will again, but it will be different. Your journey is only just beginning, my friend."

At the time, I thought that I had no talent or ability to channel information from beyond and envisioned that Guðbjörg would channel information to me that I would then use to write the books. So I decided to ask for it right there and then. "It would be nice to be able to get the material for the books directly."

They replied, "You will. We'll take care of it. We'll help you open up so that you receive it directly."

I did not understand what was said there, that I myself would receive information and channel it into books. "Will I have spiritual guides who follow me and help me?"

"We are your guides. We are with you now, friend."

I was very surprised and didn't know what to say.

"This is a turning point in your life," they said. "What you have done so far is only a prelude to what is to come. Now you will help people and make a difference with books and lectures. Remember that you will never be alone. We are always with you. You have nothing to fear regarding this. Everything will work out. You only have to trust. We teach people about eternity, eternal life, and ridding themselves of fear."

"This is very interesting and exciting," I thought to myself. "Can I ask a question?" I said after a long silence.

"Go ahead, friend" was the answer.

"Are the monks from Tibet who were here last time here now?"

Guðbjörg put her hand in the air, snapped her fingers together, and said, "Let's have them join us. Come on in." After a short while they were there, although I couldn't see them. "They're here. They smell strange, sort of like incense," said Guðbjörg.

I sensed little but listened with devotion and asked, "Are they also my spiritual guides?"

Guðbjörg cleared her throat. "They're your soul friends from the past. You were all together in Tibet in a previous life, and the souls agreed to stick together and help each other. They are cheering and rejoicing right here next to you over the fact that you are back on this spiritual path. You were their spiritual master and mentor in the monastery.

"That's why I've always found monastic life, especially in Tibet, to be so fascinating," I thought to myself while taking it all in.

When Guðbjörg had channeled to me for about an hour and a half, it was time to stop. I thanked Guðbjörg and said goodbye with a warm hug.

While I was driving home from the meeting, many thoughts went through my head. It was all so interesting and exciting. During this meeting, I had come into contact with the Tibetan monks and my spiritual guides who were going to aid me in my spiritual work. "They must be in the casual plane like Ásgeir," I reasoned. If Ásgeir are priests and storytellers, and Guðbjörg connects with the storytellers, then my guides must be scholars or kings. At the time, everything seemed so hazy and unclear, and I filled in the gaps with the information I needed. I was curious about who they were and how I could connect with them to channel information from them to people.

Then I didn't sense or see at all what was beyond, but after this meeting with Guðbjörg, I started talking to my guides. I often did so aloud while I was alone in the car or during my solitary walks in nature. I asked them to help me connect with them so that we could work together through my body to do good here on Earth. We could help people get rid of their anxiety and fear and educate and inform them about themselves, life, and their existence. I asked the guides many times to give me a name I could use to call to them, and I did my best to clear my mind so that I could receive and perceive the information. When I came home from one of my walks, I had five different names. "I have no perception or ability to receive information from beyond," I concluded.

I decided to call the monks Tíbert, and I used that name when I talked to them. Although I received little information from them, I felt a sense of calm and balance while I was talking to my guides and the monks. I thought I knew that I had no talent or ability to channel information to people, but I had developed a strong longing to be able to do so. I saw that this was the way to help people. "How can I learn this? I need to learn and master this," I thought.

I was well on my way to finding a means to build up our spiritual work and to start a spiritual center or school. This occupied my whole mind, and I didn't think about anything else during my walks. I continued writing the book, and it went well. It was as if the plot took shape by itself, and the story and the book developed in a completely different direction than I had initially planned. While I was writing, I was so immersed in the narrative that I saw myself as one of the characters and as a part of the story.

I was often anxious and felt bad during this time even though I had started my spiritual journey. I felt a greater imbalance inside me than before, and my mood swings were more intense now. I had a strong desire to withdraw from people, and I often considered if it would be best to find a small, secluded cabin to live away from everything and enjoy a simple life. "Maybe I should go to Tibet and join a monastery?" I asked myself.

My mind was in no way on the company and the lighting shop. I had worked for a long time as a subcontractor in Norway and knew little about the day-to-day operations of the company, and my interest had been fading for a long time. I now knew in my heart that I had to end my relationship with my business partner and take a different path in life. It was difficult telling my partner that I would leave the company and would instead write books and teach about spirituality. The separation was difficult and took several months to finalize. But I knew in my heart that I was doing the right thing and that this was the next step for me.

Halldóra and I founded a company for our spiritual work that was taking off, and I continued working as a subcontractor for the company in Norway. I kept writing, and the book came along well. I went on more and more walks, and they were very important to me at that time. Sometimes I cleared my mind, and sometimes I talked to my guides and Tíbert and asked for help and guidance with our spiritual work. My deepest desire was to connect more deeply with them.

The separation from the company and my business partner was difficult, and I felt a lot of anxiety and imbalance. In one of the meetings with Guðbjörg, she gave me an audio recording where she channeled Mírenda, who is the equivalent of the Virgin Mary. It was about forty-five minutes long and full of love. In it, Mírenda talked about what was in store for the Earth and what each one of us holds on the inside. The recording is from 1996, and most of what she talked about has come true. Guðbjörg told me to listen to the recording once a day for a few weeks. That would balance my nervous system, and my cellular system would become more active. I had little faith in this when Guðbjörg handed me the recording. "How can listening to something help me feel better?" I asked myself when I received the recording.

A few weeks later when I was feeling very sick and anxious, I thought I might as well give it a try and see if it couldn't help me feel better. Halldóra and I made ourselves comfortable on the sofa and started listening. I immediately felt a calmness come over me, and I grew more and more sleepy. Eventually, I fell asleep. When I woke up, the recording was long over, and it was as if I had slept through the night. Halldóra had the same experience. The next day, we did the same thing. Again, I fell asleep soon after the recording started and slept for a good while. After this had happened several days in a row, I decided to call Guðbjörg and ask her if this was intended.

"Yes," she answered on the phone. "You're supposed to fall asleep the first few times you listen because then the energy in the recording starts to heal you. When your nervous system and body are more balanced, you'll be able to listen to the entire recording without falling asleep. Keep listening every day. You're doing everything right," Guðbjörg said.

I listened every day and slowly started to feel a difference within myself and in the way I felt. The anxiety eased, and things began to settle inside me. But it happened very slowly. I had become convinced that it was helping me, so I continued to listen to the recording every day. Then, many weeks later, I managed to listen to the entire recording without falling asleep. "I'm making progress," I told myself.

My interest in spirituality grew day by day, and I started studying it on the internet. I saw a lot of new things that were unknown to me before: meditation, yoga, Reiki, healing, energy centers, kundalini energy, spiritual awakening, and higher consciousness. It was all very exciting, and I began to study these concepts. However, my main desire was to be able to connect with my guides and channel information from them, like Guðbjörg did with Ásgeir.

I started meditating, and I got comfortable in a good chair and closed my eyes. I tried my best to relax my body and breathe slowly in and out. I decided to do it for ten minutes at first and then increase the time every day. The first meditations were done more from duty than desire. I felt a little relaxation in my body but experienced more discomfort. I felt a sting in my back, the chair was uncomfortable, I itched everywhere, and those minutes were never going to pass. That was the fear and ego within me holding me back. I continued practicing every day for some time. After a few weeks, I started to feel a little pressure at the top of my head.

When I sat down to start writing, I often felt kind of empty and wouldn't know what to write. But when I closed my eyes for a moment and took a few slow breaths, I got going and the words flowed freely. Sometimes, I wasn't quick enough to write down what came to my mind. The walks started to get longer, as did the conversations with my guides. I asked them to help me make a difference, to help me help others. Every time I spoke to them, I did so aloud. I tried my best to clear my mind so that I could receive messages from them during my walks, but it didn't go well. I couldn't calm my wandering mind. Yet I felt that the walks had a good and calming effect on me. They reduced my anxiety and worry about everyday life, and writing was easier after taking a walk.

Halldóra and I had started looking around for suitable housing for our spiritual school and drove around the countryside surrounding the city. We wanted to have the school close to the city for our students' sake. We went on many day trips out of the city. One weekend we visited our youngest son, who was a manager at a hotel not far from the city. We told him that we were going to start a spiritual school to help people feel better and were looking for suitable accommodation. Somewhere with a good classroom and housing for about ten people.

Our son immediately liked the idea and said, "There is a great need for that now. So many people suffer from anxiety and stress." It was nice to see and hear how positively he received our ideas. He smiled and said, "I know of a house that suits your ideas. There's a large single-family house by Esja that is available for rent. It has two large living rooms downstairs and five bedrooms and a huge hall on the upper floor. You can rent it with furniture and chairs for lectures and a sound system."

That sounded good. "Is it available?" I asked.

"Yes, the building is owned by a company, and it isn't currently in use. So they want to rent it out to the right people. I know the man who's trying to find tenants. I'll contact him so that you can meet him to see if you get along."

It sounded good and was exciting. A few days later, our son contacted us and said we could meet the man at the house and discuss what we wanted to do there. Then the matter would be discussed at a company meeting, and a decision would be made as to whether the company wanted to rent it to us or not. We met the man and then drove to Kistufell, which lay in beautiful countryside by Esja, about a twenty-minute drive from Reykjavík. The last stretch was a bumpy dirt road.

I sensed that I was in the countryside even though we were right on the city limits. There was a beautiful view of the city from the house. We walked to the house and knocked on the door. The man greeted and welcomed us. He took us around the house, and there was a nice big kitchen downstairs, two sizable living rooms, and five bedrooms with two to three beds in each room. There was also a bathroom with a shower and a laundry room. Upstairs there was a small toilet, a large bedroom, and a large hall in the attic. There were about forty chairs and a few tables and then speakers and a sound system for lectures and teaching.

We liked the house, as it was exactly what we were looking for. We went over what we were going to do in the house: let people come to us for a few days to disconnect from the hustle and bustle of everyday life, get out of the city, enjoy the countryside, learn about themselves, and learn to relax. The agenda was not firmly established at this stage. The man listened to us and liked our ideas. We said we were thinking of living in the upstairs room ourselves. So it would be a home and a school in the same place. He said he would have to present this at the company meeting, and then he would contact us. We were excited and hoped that this would work out.

A few days later, we were contacted and informed that we could rent the house, but they would have to use it for a few weeks during the summer. We agreed to this and signed the lease. We received the keys at the beginning of January 2016.

I continued writing the book *Konungur án Krúnu* (*King without a Crown*), and at the same time, I started to set up a website for the school and had a suitable logo designed and made. We planned to advertise ourselves and present the events that would be available on the website. We were making good progress in getting our school up and running. We went to Guðbjörg, and she said she would join us there at the school and help us get this started. She would hold classes and teach. That sounded good and was a great support for our work.

In November 2015, the manuscript for my first book was ready. It was a strange feeling when I sat and wrote the concluding chapter and finally put down the last period in the story. I felt like I was saying goodbye to dear friends and that I had lived in the world of the story and was closely connected to the main characters to whom I was now saying goodbye. I felt a lot of emptiness, longing, and regret. It was a memorable feeling that I did not expect. I thought I would feel a sense of victory and joy at finishing the book, but I didn't.

I started looking for a proofreader to review the text, and I finally found a woman who was willing to do the job for me. I sent her the manuscript, and a few weeks later, she said she was ready and wanted to meet me at a coffee shop to go over the project and the book. I was very excited to hear what she thought of the book. I met her at a coffee shop a few days later. We had coffee, and I told her about myself and what my wife and I were doing.

After staying silent for a while, she said, "This is a very interesting book; I had to read it twice. It's a very heartwarming story that makes you feel good, and reading it calmed me down."

I was happy to hear this, which is what I was hoping for: that the book created a sense of calm and well-being for the reader. She handed me a flash drive and said it contained the book with her suggestions for corrections. I could decide whether to follow them or not.

"Will you bring the book to a publisher or publish it yourself?" she asked after handing me the flash drive.

"I'm not really sure; I'll have to look into it some more," I replied.

She got up, shook my hand, and said goodbye, wishing me luck with the book. I thanked her profusely.

I decided to publish the book myself and sell it to those who came to our courses. I contacted printers in Iceland and quickly found that it was expensive to get the book printed in the country. Therefore, I started looking for printing services abroad and finally found a printer in Ljubljana, Slovenia, who was willing to help me. I wanted five hundred copies printed, but I negotiated to have one thousand copies printed since this option was not significantly more expensive. We were informed that the book could be printed in the spring, and we agreed that we would visit the printing house in the spring to go over the project. Our older son is a trained printer and helped me prepare the book for printing.

We moved to Kistufell in early February 2016, by which point we had rented out our apartment in Reykjavík. Kistufell was in a beautiful place, but it was often windy there next to Esja and was rarely calm.

The Spiritual Work Begins

I started going for walks in the surroundings of Kistufell. There were large fields that were nice to walk around, and most of the time I walked all the way up to the mountain Esja. There was also a beautiful stream that ran through the fields. The view was beautiful when I walked back to the house, the city appearing as well as a view of the sea. During these walks, I talked to my spiritual guides and asked for help and guidance in connecting with them and being able to channel information and education from them. I often sat by the stream and took a deep breath, relaxed, and cleared my mind. All I could hear was the sound of the stream, and it was a good place for meditation. I forgot time and place while sitting there in nature.

Shortly after we moved to Kistufell, Guðbjörg suggested holding a four-day spiritual course there, for Halldóra and me and another couple. The couple could stay with us, and Guðbjörg would teach us during the day. We liked the idea, and the couple arrived on a Thursday. Guðbjörg taught us meditations to increase our sensitivity and intuition. I quickly sensed that the exercises were fatiguing. In the evenings we cooked and ate together, and there was plenty to talk about. I had a good time with them. It was nice to meet other people who were spiritually minded and be able to share views and perspectives.

Then came one exercise where we were to channel for each other. Guðbjörg asked me to practice with the woman, and she started channeling to me. I asked a lot about my spiritual guides, and she told me that I would write many books in the future and that I would connect with my guides. She was obviously not channeling for the first time, and it was easy for her. She was very sensitive and had a good connection. Then Guðbjörg said, "That's enough. Now we switch, and Viktor will channel to her."

I felt my stomach curl up with anxiety. "I don't know anything about it. I have never done that before," I answered weakly.

But the woman smiled and said kindly, "I will help you. It will be alright." She said this so gently that I calmed down and gained courage.

"If I am going to learn this and run a spiritual school, I will have to make the leap," I thought to myself.

"You close your eyes and breathe slowly, take a deep breath, relax, and say the first thing that comes to you when she asks you something," Guðbjörg said and patted me on the shoulder. Then she walked over to Halldóra and the man, who were doing the same exercise.

I started to relax and close my eyes. When I was ready, the woman started asking me questions. Every time she finished a question, I visualized pictures and then described them to her as best I could.

Spiritual Awakening

"That's right. It fits," the woman said when I had finished describing what I saw and sensed. These words encouraged me and gave me the strength and courage to continue. "Do you see my dog?"

I waited a moment, then saw a black Labrador dog standing close to the woman's side, and I saw how the dog followed her wherever she went. I saw that the dog had a purple collar. I explained all this to the woman, and when I finished channeling and opened my eyes, I saw that the woman was smiling. "Was that right?" I asked hastily.

"Everything checks out. I have a black Labrador bitch who is very dear to me and follows me everywhere, and she has a purple collar."

I was very proud of myself. "I can channel," I thought to myself.

Guðbjörg came to us and said, "How did he do?"

The woman smiled. "He did great. It went really well."

Guðbjörg put her hand on my shoulder and said, "Good boy."

We all got up and Guðbjörg said, "Well, today's program is over. Let's see to dinner." We went down to the kitchen and started making dinner. I was so proud of myself that I thought about little else but my performance channeling.

Guðbjörg taught us all day, with breaks in between. We had a lot to learn and practiced healing and seeing the color of each other's aura. Then we meditated a lot. I felt pressure at the top of my head when meditating, and I couldn't relax properly. When we sat and ate lunch on the final day of the course, Guðbjörg said, "After dinner, I'm going to channel Mírenda to you and then the course is finished. How does that sound?" We all answered in unison, "Very well."

I had listened to the recording of Mírenda many times, so I was eager to see and hear Guðbjörg channel her directly for us. When we had finished eating and tidied up after dinner, we went upstairs to the hall. We got chairs and lined ourselves up in front of the stage. Guðbjörg took off her glasses and stood in front of us, looking at us in turn with a smile on her face. She started inhaling deeply through her nose, and I could see her abdomen expanding. Guðbjörg's face changed and her eyes became like piercing stars, and suddenly Guðbjörg said in a gentle but firm voice, "Welcome, my name is Mírenda. My dear friends, you are wonderful souls."

It was a special experience to see and hear Mírenda right there in front of us after having listened to the recording so many times. Mírenda spoke to each of the others, and then it was my turn. She was now standing in front of me and looking deep into my eyes. I felt how it affected my heart and emotions. I felt the love in my heart, and I felt my eyes start to fill with tears from the love I sensed. Then she started talking to me. "Dear friend, you are a brave soul. You will do well, and your dreams will come true." I could feel the tears rolling down my cheeks as she continued. "You will become connected, and your school will grow day by day. Be brave and patient and it will all become reality, my dear friend." I didn't say a word—I only watched and listened in amazement at what was happening.

When Guðbjörg had disconnected, she smiled and said, "That was Mírenda."

We all sat there and stared at Guðbjörg. No one could say a word. Finally I said, "That was an amazing experience." We all marveled at what had happened. "That was a great experience," I said to the group as we walked down to the kitchen.

We had coffee after the meeting, and then the people started to pack their things and get ready to go home. Halldóra and I stood by the front door and watched the cars drive away. Guðbjörg went first, the couple following. We closed the door and went inside. I felt a great emptiness in my heart when they were all gone. I felt a bit sad and empty inside; it had been a wonderful time and a great experience, and I had learned a lot. But now I would return to my normal life. The next morning, as I was working at the computer, I kept thinking about what I had experienced and learned during the course.

A few days later, Halldóra and I went to Guðbjörg. We talked about the course and what happened there, but then Guðbjörg said, "Viktor, you have a strong calling to help people. We can feel and sense it in your heart a mile away." She looked at me for a long time. "A lot is changing in your life," she added. "Your life thus far and the past are just a prelude and preparation for what is to come. You came to Earth to help and teach people, and your time has come. We will help you and prepare you for the work to come."

I listened carefully to what Guðbjörg said, and my heart was filled with great joy and anticipation. I sensed that what she said was true. There was no turning back.

Guðbjörg looked at me with a smile and said, "I have a doctor who works with me on the other side. His name is Jonathan, and he wants to see you." Guðbjörg started to get comfortable in the chair.

"That's exciting," I said.

Guðbjörg quickly connected to Jónatan, and he had the same voice as Ásgeir, but spoke more lightly. "Hello, my dear couple," said Jonatan. "Can I clean you out and open the energy pathways in your body?"

We both agreed, and Guðbjörg got up and pushed away the table that stood between us. "I need to be able to access you better," said Jonathan as he walked over to us. "Close your eyes and take a deep breath. I'm going to wash away the dirty energy in you." He started swinging his hands rapidly in front of my chest as if he was pulling something out. He did this alternately with me and Halldóra. "You need to learn to stop taking in this filth from your surroundings and from other people. It only creates anxiety and worry for you. Your body is not a trash can," said Jonathan playfully. He continued for a long time and then went to the head. "There is a lot here too that needs to be released."

Jonathan worked on us for a long time, but then Guðbjörg sat down and broke the connection and said, "There was a lot that came out of you. I need to go clean. It would be best to take a shower. This energy clings to me." She went out of the room, and when she returned to the living room, she sat down in front of us. "Jonathan helps us open up our bodies, cleans the energy channels, and clears out dirty energy. The body needs to be clean so you can receive new energy to channel. You should rest today and drink a lot of water. You will feel tired for a few days afterward. It's all normal. It is a great struggle for the body to replace the energy."

After the meeting, we said thanks and followed Guðbjörg's advice. We drove home to Kistufell and rested for what remained of the day. I felt very tired the next day. I felt like I had been working for a long time without rest. "This seems to be working," I thought to myself. I went for long walks around the countryside every day and enjoyed myself alone in nature. I talked to my spiritual guides and asked for help so that I could do my best and help people. I didn't feel ready or able to start teaching people. I was often anxious, and I felt conflicted inside. At that time, I felt best when I was alone. There was often a doubt in my mind about whether I had the ability to channel information. Souls who are scholars and kings are too earthbound to channel. That's why I often thought, "IF I get through and IF I get a connection." I later learned that these are not the right thoughts to have when embarking on a project or a journey, because doubt hinders progress and causes delays.

A week later we went back to Guðbjörg, and when we had made ourselves comfortable on the sofa, she said, "I was thinking we should promote the house and what you do and hold a decent-sized séance. We can advertise it and fill the house. I can channel and you can take care of the coffee for the people who come. What do you think?"

We looked at each other and then at Guðbjörg. "This is a great idea," I answered, looking at Halldóra.

"We like the idea," answered Halldóra.

Then it was decided. I posted the event on our website, and we advertised the gathering on the radio. It was strange to hear it announced on the radio. Halldóra and I went and bought coffee and tea. I lined up chairs in the hall in the loft and tested the sound system. Everything was ready when Guðbjörg arrived. I greeted her with a hug and welcomed her. "Now things are really happening," I thought to myself.

"Are you ready?" I asked Guðbjörg when she sat down in the kitchen.

She smiled. "You bet," she replied. "This will be fun."

I looked out the kitchen window and saw a few cars in the distance coming along the driveway. "There, the first guests are arriving," I said excitedly, looking to Guðbjörg and Halldóra, who were sitting at the kitchen table.

"You should greet them," said Guðbjörg, adding, "Welcome them and direct them to their seats here in the living room to begin with."

I was excited and a little shy when I opened the door to greet the guests, but I welcomed the people and showed them into the living room, which seated about fifteen people. Then more and more people came, and I went to the door and greeted each guest one after the other. I started showing the people the house and told them about the work we were going to do. Most people seemed positive and enthusiastic.

Guðbjörg had started walking around to introduce herself. Some knew Guðbjörg and had visited her before. When it was ten minutes to seven, Guðbjörg said loudly, "Well, everyone, the séance starts in ten minutes. Let's go upstairs and get ready." People were still arriving, and I saw that I needed to add and arrange more chairs in the hall.

The people took their seats and settled down, and after a short while the hall was quiet. Guðbjörg sat on a chair in the innermost part of the room and calmly looked over the group. There were forty people present at our first séance at Kistufell. Guðbjörg stood up and introduced herself. "My name is Guðbjörg Sveinsdóttir, and I have worked as a medium for over twenty years. I learned the practice with Reverend Sigurður Haukur and stayed with him for some time, and soon I started channeling Ásgeir, who is a teacher from the casual plane. They are a group of about a thousand souls who have become a whole. They possess a lot of knowledge and wisdom. They are not fortune tellers, but they help people and educate and make good therapists.

"They asked me in the beginning if I wanted to work with them and said they would make sure that I would never be poor and never rich but always have enough to eat and have shelter, be able to pay my bills, and be carefree. I accepted this, and it has worked out all this time. You can ask Ásgeir about anything, anything you can think of, but it is best to keep the questions concise because then you will get concise answers."

The people listened attentively to Guðbjörg. I watched closely and stood at the back of the hall making sure everything was OK. Guðbjörg stopped speaking and looked across the room. Then an older woman sitting in the front of the hall said, "I thought I was going to a séance." It was clear that she was hoping for dead relatives and friends to be channeled.

It was as if Guðbjörg didn't hear her as she continued. "I also have a doctor, Jonathan. He helps people and is a healer. He is playful and funny and can be a bit of a womanizer. I intend to start by channeling him, and then I can walk among you. But later I will channel Ásgeir, and then I have to sit in the chair there."

The older woman was clearly disappointed with the meeting and repeated, "I thought this was a séance."

Guðbjörg looked at the woman. "You can leave if you are unhappy. Go ahead," Guðbjörg said, and pointed toward the door. The woman sat firm, unmoving.

Guðbjörg continued as if nothing had happened. "Now I'm going to get Jonathan. He will walk among you and talk to you and help those who want help and give permission."

I continued to follow everything that happened. Guðbjörg quickly bonded with Jonathan. One hand swayed slightly, and she arched her back and began to stagger forward into the hall. He began by walking over to the woman who had been calling for a séance. "Hello, friend," Jonathan said and stood in front of the woman, who looked up but did not answer. "Can we take a look at you?" he asked and smiled.

She answered softly: "Yes."

Jonatan placed his hand on one of the woman's shoulders and said, "The boy will be alright. Everything will be fine."

The woman looked up. "Boy? What are you talking about?" the woman replied, a bit sharply.

"Isn't your son having surgery soon? We just meant that everything will go well and he will make a full recovery."

The woman looked up at Jonathan. "Thank you, that's good to hear. It's a great relief. I've been worrying about this for a long time."

Jonathan remained by the woman's side and said, "You came here tonight to get this information. That was your purpose for coming here. Are you happy with this?" Jonathan lightly tapped the woman's shoulder.

"Yes, I am happy to hear this," she said. "It's a great relief."

Jonathan smiled. "That's good to hear, my dear friend."

Jonathan went to more guests and talked to them and helped them. I watched everything. "This job takes a lot of guts and courage," I thought to myself.

After this, we took a break. Halldóra had already heated water for tea and prepared coffee for everyone. After the break, Guðbjörg sat down in a chair in front of the crowd and said she would channel Ásgeir. In a short while he came through, and Guðbjörg spoke in a dark and husky voice. Ásgeir invited people to ask questions. The people asked very different questions, and Ásgeir answered them all.

When the meeting concluded, the people immediately started leaving. Halldóra, Guðbjörg, and I stood by the kitchen window and watched the last cars pull out of the driveway. We had a cup of coffee together before Guðbjörg headed home after a successful evening.

A few days later, the printing house in Slovenia contacted me and told me that they would soon be printing our book. I contacted them, and it was decided that we would visit them to decide on the paper and texture of the book. They were also going to design the cover and set it up for us. I had asked Halldóra's niece to draw a picture that I wanted to have on the front page. She was studying art, and it was fun to have her join us for the project. I put together three proposals for a cover and sent them to the printing house.

Halldóra and I invited Guðbjörg to come with us on the trip to Slovenia, and she gratefully accepted. We first flew to Copenhagen, where we had a wonderful time together for part of the day. The next morning we flew to Ljubljana, Slovenia. We started out by going to a hotel that was on Lake Bled. "This is paradise on Earth," I said, as we could see the water through the car window. A small island in the middle of the lake was prominent, with a church tower towering over it. There was a beautiful mountain view all around the lake. We stayed in a hotel that faced the lake and had a view of it from the balcony. We stayed there for a few days before our meeting with the printing house.

When the time came, we drove to the capital and to the printing house. It was an exciting time. "Finally, the book will be in print," I thought to myself as we entered the building. Two people welcomed us and went over the project with us. I wanted the paper to be a little yellowish, and they quickly brought a sample. When we had agreed on the paper, we were invited into an office, where one of the employees showed us suggestions for the book cover on a computer screen. "Here are three suggestions I made according to your instructions," said the employee. There was the drawing on the cover and the blue color I had chosen. When we were done looking at the suggestions, the man said, "Since this is a spiritual book, I decided to make one suggestion myself." It was a brownish cover with golden sunrays coming down the page, and the title was golden as well. We all agreed that this was the one and was much better suited than the blue color. This meant that the hand-painted image that was supposed to be on the front cover was now on the back. I wasn't quite happy with that at first, but eventually I accepted the cover that he had suggested. We then concluded the contract, and they estimated that the book would be ready in about three weeks. They would then ship it to our home in Kistufell. The next day we headed home to Iceland after an all-around successful trip.

It was around this time that I started having very vivid and intense dreams. Many of them were so real that I could not distinguish them from reality. Usually, I received strong messages in the dreams, and they were my encouragement and guidance. Colors were always very prominent in these dreams. They would be very strong and deep. In one of the first ones, I was in a small, windowless room with a tiny sofa, a small desk, and a chair. The room was green. "Where am I now?" I asked myself as I looked around. I sat down on the couch and decided to wait. After a while, I could hear people talking on the other side of the wall. It seemed as if the number of people grew little by little, and eventually it became a large and dense crowd. I started to get restless because I finally realized that it was I who was supposed to give a lecture to all these people who had gathered there. I started pacing the floor back and forth. Then I heard someone say to me, "Dear friend, calm down. There is nothing to fear. We are with you and will always be with you." I looked up. These are my spiritual guides, I realized. They are with me and will be with me. I felt my fear and anxiety go away, and I gained strength and courage. "It's time," I thought to myself as I opened the door and walked down the hall toward the stage. Then I woke up.

Guðbjörg started holding courses with us at Kistufell. She offered two types of courses—Sensitivity and Intuition was intended for beginners, and Opening to Mediumship was for more advanced students. Halldóra and I participated in these courses like the other students. The courses were held on Friday evenings from eight to midnight, and then the second part was held on Saturday from ten to two. Often the students stayed over at Kistufell and ate breakfast with us. I usually felt exhausted after these classes and was exhausted for several days afterward. Guðbjörg told me that the fatigue was in fact progress. The energy was being worked, and it was intense for the body. It was being cleared out to make room for new energy. I felt that my perception was lacking and limited, and at times I seriously doubted that I had any ability to become a spiritual teacher and mentor.

At one course, opening to mediumship, ten students attended and Guðbjörg taught and guided. After we had gone to meditation to get us going, Guðbjörg split us up so that two and two had to work together and channel for each other. We spread out all over the hall so that there was a good distance between us so as not to disturb each other. Then Guðbjörg stepped in and guided us. I met a young man who was a beginner like me. "Please go ahead," Guðbjörg said to the group.

"I don't know anything about this," I said to the man with a smile.

He looked at me and said, "Me neither. Let's try our best."

Instead of channeling for the man, I got curious and started listening to what the others were doing in the hall. I heard that many people were busy channeling, and I looked up and across the hall and saw that everyone had already begun. I was filled with hopelessness. "I'll never make it," I thought to myself. Finally, Guðbjörg came to us and asked how things were going.

"It's not working," I replied.

"Just start talking to him. You're already overshadowed," Guðbjörg said. She started swinging her hand at my chest as if she was pulling something out. "Now I'm easing the energy. Just start talking and everything will start. You can do it." Then Guðbjörg went to the other students.

I could not channel this time, and the course was very disappointing to me. My mind was full of doubts about whether I could do this, and they dragged me down, but there was something in my chest that still encouraged me to continue my journey.

Finally, the book *King Without a Crown* came from the printing house. The books came in small cardboard boxes stacked on a pallet. There was great anticipation when Halldóra and I went out to look at the pallet and the books. I felt great joy and a feeling of victory when I opened the first box and got to touch the first book. "It's finally in print," I thought to myself.

We began working on selling and marketing the book. I sent one copy to the City Library and to the largest bookstore chain. Within a few days, I received a reply that the library wanted to buy twelve copies, and then I received a list of stores willing to sell the book. Halldóra and I drove the book to most bookstores in the capital area and sent a few copies to the countryside. In the first few months we sold a few dozen books.

I started putting together lectures and tutorials so I could start teaching and helping people. I put together a course in spiritual studies where I taught about the soul age, soul role, and personality. I started preparing slides on the computer, which I showed on a screen using a projector. I also put together other lectures, such as "Life between Lives." I started advertising on our website and elsewhere online. At first, three to four people came to each lecture, and some bought a book. Gradually, the number of people decreased until finally no one came. Sometimes I would stand at the kitchen window and look out into the driveway a few minutes before the advertised lecture was due to start, but no one came.

One day the postman came with a package, and when I opened it, I saw that it was one of the bookstores returning unsold books to us. Later that evening, no one came to a lecture we had advertised online. I went to Halldóra and said, "This won't work. I can't get this started. It is best to give this up and move back home to our apartment."

Halldóra hugged me and reassured me. "You can do this. It just takes time."

I calmed down hearing this, and hope rekindled in my chest.

A woman who had been with Guðbjörg a lot and who had visited us several times at Kistufell had given me a copy of Paramahansa Yogananda's autobiography. The book was in English and is called *Autobiography of a Yogi*. On the cover of the book was Yogananda in an orange robe with black hair. Guðbjörg had told me that I should not read spiritual books; it would only interfere with my channeling in the future. The knowledge would come from my spiritual guides. "You don't need any books," she had said. But I got permission and an exemption to read this book.

Sometimes I lay on the sofa at Kistufell and read the book, which was very interesting. "Yogananda was a great spiritual master," I thought to myself. I noticed that just before he began to study with his guru and work on himself, he had a great desire to run away to the mountains. He went and met an old man who told him that he would not find God in a cave in a mountain but with the help of his guru. So Yogananda turned around and went back to his guru and started studying with him. I recognized this feeling when I wanted to retire and move to a small hut in some remote place. After he had studied with his guru, he moved from his native India to the United States and began to make a name for himself there, lecturing around the country. His work started slowly, but later thousands of people started attending his lectures. Finally, he founded a spiritual school that is still active today in many parts of the world.

When the people stopped coming to my lectures and the book sales started shrinking and I couldn't connect with my guides and my hope was failing, I had a dream that gave me motivation to continue. It was one of those lucid and realistic dreams I had started having. I dreamed that I was sitting at the back of the hall at Kistufell. I looked out into the hall. A few meters in front of me stood a man with his back to me; he was wearing an orange tunic and had long, obsidian-black hair. I had never seen an orange so deep and vivid nor a black color so black as there. The colors on his tunic and in his hair were memorable, strong, and deep. I got up from the chair and started walking slowly toward the man, and as I got closer I heard him talking. He didn't seem to notice me as I came up behind him. Finally, I stood next to him, and then I saw that in front of him sat a man and a woman listening to the man, who seemed to be teaching or lecturing. Eventually he stopped talking and slowly turned to me, and I saw that it was Yogananda. He said to me, "You can see only two people came to my lecture. That's how it was for me in the beginning. Be brave and patient, and gradually more people will come to your lectures."

Ragnar Viktor Karlsson

I sensed when I woke up that it was a strong message dream, and it gave me a lot of hope and wind in my sails. I had received the spark to keep going.

I had taken part in several courses with Guðbjörg, and I showed little or no progress. "You should have made great progress," said Guðbjörg, and it seemed as if she was giving up on teaching me. It was then, in October 2016, that she called me and told me that she didn't have the energy to do this anymore. She was going to leave us at Kistufell and take a break from teaching me. Finally, she said to me on the phone, "Let's talk again in the new year." I said goodbye and hung up and looked out into the darkness from the living room at Kistufell. Outside there was a storm.

It was a terrible experience and a big shock. I was filled with anxiety and felt a great discomfort in my chest. I sat down in the living room and thought about what to do. "Perhaps my determination is being tested," I thought to myself. I worked in the Norwegian job as before and thought next to nothing about spiritual matters until Christmas.

On Christmas Day 2016, I was lying on the sofa. I started thinking about the spiritual issues, and there was a great desire and calling inside me to continue. While I was meditating on this, I felt a light energy coming over my head. This energy made me feel good. It freed me of anxiety and fear, and I managed to relax. This energy was a taste of what I had experienced some time before. "This is a calling to continue," I thought to myself as I sat up on

144

the couch. From that day on, this energy started coming to me and over me regularly. I sensed it mostly above my head. The energy made me feel at ease and took away all my tension and fear. After the end of the year, I called Guðbjörg and said I wanted to continue working on the connection with my spiritual guides. Guðbjörg was happy to hear that, and we decided that I would come to her regularly for private lessons. Until now, I had met Guðbjörg irregularly, mostly during the courses she had held with us in Kistufell. Now I was going to take this seriously and have a regular appointment with her every week.

Around the time I was starting with Guðbjörg, I had one of my strong message dreams. I was walking through grassy fields and meadows, and I walked for a long time until I came to a grassy slope. The slope seemed very long, and I had a hard time seeing the end of it. I slowly walked up the hill, where you could see tall, old trees standing scattered. The colors were vivid and deep. I had never seen the grass so green, and the sky was a beautiful blue with just a few wisps of white clouds. I contemplated all this as I continued my walk up the hill. Finally, I spotted a bulge up ahead. I didn't see what it was at first because it was far, far away. I continued, and gradually the picture became clearer. There was a long-haired man sitting on a gray stone wearing a white tunic, his back turned to me. He was sitting on the edge of a mountain that was at the top of the slope, and as I got closer I could hear him talking. I walked all the way to him and finally stood next to him and calmly looked down at him. He slowly turned his head toward me, and then I saw that it was Jesus sitting there.

He stood up, put his hands on my shoulders, and said, "Welcome, my dear friend. I have been waiting for you." I stood there speechless. I felt great love in his presence. After a short while, he looked over the edge and said, "Look here." I looked over the edge, and I was surprised because there was a huge sea of people as far as the eye could see in all directions. Then he looked at me and said, "It's your turn." He pointed to the rock where he had been sitting. Then he started walking down the hill from where I came. I looked alternately at him walking away and at the rock and at the sea of people before me. I felt like it was all of humanity standing there in front of me. Slowly, Jesus disappeared from my sight, and I stood there by the rock looking alternately at the rock and the sea of people until I woke up.

A few days later, it was time for my first appointment with Guðbjörg. I drove to her place, and as I was walking from the car to the house, I was filled with anxiety and fear. I didn't know what to expect and feared the unknown. I thought she would snap a finger and I would be able to connect with my spiritual guides just like that. "Will I make a connection today?" I wondered to myself as I rang the doorbell. She greeted me with a smile, but I was apprehensive when I walked in and sat down on the sofa in front of her. She sat in a chair across from me, a coffee table between us.

"Would you like some coffee before we start?"

Spiritual Awakening

I agreed, and she got us each a cup of coffee from the kitchen. Guðbjörg looked at me for a long time while we drank the coffee. I recalled the first time I sat there on the sofa and had a long list of questions for Ásgeir. Now I was empty and had no questions and little to say.

"Well, my dear Viktor," Guðbjörg said. "What can you tell me about your childhood and upbringing?"

At first I didn't understand what this was all about and how it was related to the connection that I had come to establish. Gradually, I realized that this was part of the cleansing and coming to terms with the past—which is the key to progress, as it creates space for new energy. I started going over my early years and my childhood. In my mind, my childhood was without major conflict, and I felt how my mother and grandmother had been good to me and helped me grow up and taught me to distinguish right from wrong. "I see now I should be grateful for growing up with good and loving people. It is the foundation for my life," I said to Guðbjörg after I had told her the outlines of my childhood.

"Very true," she replied.

I could feel how I calmed down and how the anxiety, fear, and worry disappeared from me while I was with Guðbjörg. She had a good influence on me. Guðbjörg listened attentively to the story of my upbringing and asked questions intermittently. "Are you nervous?" she asked, looking at my hands.

"It happens," I replied.

"I see you bite your nails, which makes the fingers look ugly. Do you want to look like this when you start teaching people?"

I looked at my fingers and answered, "No, this is not exemplary."

"We need to fix this. Your first piece of homework is to stop biting your nails."

I smiled. "About time after all these years," I answered. Then I added, "I'll do it."

Time passed quickly, and the session was about to end when I said, "Can I tell you about a dream I had?"

Guðbjörg adjusted in her chair. "Of course," she replied.

I began to tell her about the dream where I walked up the hill and how Jesus greeted me and told me it was my turn to teach and then disappeared down the hill, leaving me alone in front of a large crowd of people.

Guðbjörg listened carefully and then said, "This is a remarkable dream. Let it be the motivation for your journey."

My first private lesson was over. We got up, and I hugged Guðbjörg and thanked her dearly. Even though I didn't achieve the connection I was after, I gained a lot of hope. After this session, all the need and desire to bite my nails disappeared, and I have not bitten them since.

Spiritual Awakening

I continued to talk and pray to my spiritual guides during my walks. I walked a lot in the fields near Kistufell. Sometimes I walked in blowing wind and rain, and I enjoyed letting the weather wash over me.

There were some ominous signs in the Norwegian work I had been doing as a subcontractor for several years. The projects were all being completed, and few new projects came in. I was often anxious because of this and feared for the future. Soon after, I was contacted and informed that I would be let go and that I would have to come to Norway as soon as possible to return the computer and the stuff I used for my work. The news filled me with anxiety, but I immediately got to buying a plane ticket to Norway. There, I went to a meeting with my boss, where he officially informed me that they were forced to let me go due to a lack of projects. "If it's any consolation, I can tell you that it is extremely difficult for me to have to dismiss such a good engineer as you. Everyone here is happy with your work."

I looked at him and said, "Thank you. It's difficult for me to stop working here. I have felt good and worked with good people."

Finally, we got up from the table and shook hands, and I said goodbye to my colleagues in the office and walked out. I wrestled with difficult feelings as I left the building. I was full of disappointment and sadness. I took the train to the airport and flew home to Iceland.

Ragnar Viktor Karlsson

I had a fixed appointment once a week with Guðbjörg, but my sense of time was changing—sometimes I felt like I was with her every day, and sometimes it felt like there was a month between appointments. In the first few sessions, Guðbjörg began by asking me, "Who are you?"

I didn't understand this question at the time. "She knows everything about me. Why is she asking me this?" I thought to myself and looked at her for a long time, but finally I answered, "That's a good question."

I had no other answers, but she added, "Think it over on your walks."

I talked to my spiritual guides when I was alone in the car and on my walks. I asked them for help in achieving a connection with them and allowing me to share information and knowledge from them with the people so that I could have a positive impact here on Earth.

Every now and then I felt a comfortable energy above my head. Then all the anxiety, fear, and worry disappeared. I felt good with this energy and wanted more.

I started looking for a job in Iceland and immediately found one job online. The application deadline had expired, but I still decided to get in touch. The job was at an engineering firm that had its headquarters in Reykjavík and had branches all over the country. They were looking for an electrical engineer for the branch in Akranes. It suited me well because it wasn't that far from Kistufell. I went for an interview and got the job. The first few days I was at the office in Reykjavík, but then I went to Akranes.

I could choose where to work from day to day. When I had an appointment with Guðbjörg, I worked in Reykjavík. I got a good office in Akranes, where I sat alone in a room. It suited me very well as these transformations were taking place within me.

My glasses were getting old and I was having trouble reading fine print, so I went to the eye doctor and got tested and got a pair of bifocal glasses. This was a big change, as now I could read all text I encountered. A few days after I got the glasses, I suddenly had a hard time reading signs and road markings and large text. Everything seemed hazy and blurry. At first I thought my glasses were greasy, so I went into the nearest eyeglasses store and asked for help cleaning the lenses, but it didn't help. So I made an appointment with the ophthalmologist and asked him whether these glasses were the right ones and what we had ordered. The doctor checked the glasses, and they were as they should be. In the next session with Guðbjörg, I told her about this and that there was no explanation for it. She smiled and said, "You shouldn't have gone to the doctor with this, as it's related to your spiritual opening. Your body is changing, and you will experience this for a few days, then it will pass and you will see normally again."

I smiled. "I'll start by coming to you if I notice something like this in the future," I said.

Dr. Jonathan continued to extract dirty energy from me, from my throat, stomach, and chest. I sometimes had pain over my chest and neck, and sometimes it was like I had a mildly sore throat. Guðbjörg told me that this was part of the body opening up. Your frequency increases, and you steadily start pulling in higher and higher energy.

Guðbjörg and I had made several attempts to get me to channel my spiritual guides. I sat down on the couch across from her, closed my eyes, relaxed, and breathed deeply but slowly, in and out. I perceived energy that came over my head, but I did not receive any information and had nothing to say to Guðbjörg. It was all stuck and progressed little. I often lost hope, and it often occurred to me to quit. But there was something inside me that encouraged me to keep going. Guðbjörg also had a unique way of giving me hope again when it was almost completely gone. It happened several times that I was on my way to Guðbjörg and was determined to thank her and tell her that it was over, that I would not continue and that I didn't have the ability to channel or to become a spiritual teacher. But after sitting on her couch for a few minutes, I was full of hope and full of faith that I could do it and was eager to continue.

Suddenly, I began thinking a lot about Tibetan monks and Tibet. I started looking at a lot of material on the internet about Tibet and life there as a monk. I found it very fascinating and had a great desire to go there and preferably stay in a monastery for some time. During the Chinese invasion of Tibet, many monasteries were destroyed, and many of the monks fled from Tibet to Nepal and India. So I started looking for a Tibetan monastery in those parts. I started listening to mantras that came from Tibet, and they had a calming effect on me. I felt more and more distant from the Western world. The news and media created anger within me and sometimes hatred. I always saw the policies and actions of the shadow power shining through this media, and I saw how the human rights and freedoms of the people were steadily curtailed. Many people even seemed to welcome this. I was turning away from the consumerism I had been involved in and starting to strive for a simpler life instead. That's why I found life in a monastery to be more and more fascinating.

I went to the next session with Guðbjörg, and as before, I was a bit nervous while driving to her. I gradually began to notice the way she spoke and what her outlook on life was and is. She never spoke ill of any person and had great love for everyone. To me, she seemed completely free of anxiety and fear. This was the life I was after. When I had settled down on her couch, it was as if I had arrived in another world, and I felt comfortable there. I started examining myself and how I sometimes talked about other people, especially how I had sometimes talked carelessly about others and even spoken ill of them.

After a long silence, Guðbjörg said, "What are you thinking of?"

I smiled and thought, "Can she read my thoughts?" I replied, "I have noticed that you never speak ill of anyone. If you talk about someone, it's a parable, so I can learn from it. This is something I am going to adopt from this moment on. I see now that it's bad to speak ill of others. It has a bad effect on my well-being and presumably the person in question as well. I am ashamed of my past behavior."

Guðbjörg smiled. "I'm glad to hear this. These are signs of progress for you, Viktor. We are to love everything and everyone, and then we will be loved. As the Savior said, love your neighbor as yourself and also love your enemies. Be aware of your words because they are effective. We hear every word you say on the couch. What words you choose and how you say things. The words reflect the thoughts and the mind and where you are in the process.

"Your next step is to become aware of your thoughts, because they have the same effect as your words and actions. Learn to think well of others. Because bad and evil thoughts toward you and others cause you and them discomfort."

I listened to every word, and I understood and accepted it all.

"It is your homework to examine and analyze your thoughts," said Guðbjörg.

"I will," I replied.

When I was driving home from my appointment with Guðbjörg, I thought to myself, "I have made a lot of progress even though I took a small step today." I was grateful to have realized this. I felt a great relief inside me when I stopped talking carelessly and ill of others. At the same time, I also stopped judging others, even though I didn't always understand their actions. I realized that we all have different missions and challenges here on Earth. Although we aim for the same place at the end, we take different paths to the goal. If I happened to speak carelessly of others from this moment onward, I felt it stab me to the heart. I sensed how wrong it was, and I wished I could take back my words. These few accidents helped me stop it altogether. I began to examine and analyze my thoughts and began to replace negative and evil thoughts with positive and loving ones. I began to see the positive and the good in all people and in everything around me, and I became blind to the negative and bad things in other people's lives.

A few months after changing my words and thoughts to love and positivity and not speaking carelessly about others, I began to feel changes within me—specifically, I experienced more freedom and lightness. My worries were gradually evaporating, and the problems that occurred regularly were all disappearing. I was starting to feel great positive changes in my life and well-being. It was the first time I accepted that spirituality helped me feel better in my daily life. Now I was thirsty to feel better and better day by day, and it was now my motivation to continue the journey.

In the next session with Guðbjörg, I went over how I had done with the homework and told her about my improved well-being and how I felt more and more lightness inside me and less worry. Guðbjörg smiled. "I'm happy with you now. You have made progress, my friend." Then she added, "When you're ready, you'll be lecturing and teaching and guiding people, so go online and find videos of spiritual teachers and see how they carry themselves and what they're teaching. But as I have told you, do not read any more spiritual books or imitate others. Everything you will teach in the future will come directly from your spiritual guides. What you have read and looked at and what is in your mind can interfere and affect the channeling. It is best to know nothing when you start.

"That's how it was for me. I have never read spiritual books or the Bible, but I can channel information, knowledge, and wisdom to you despite that. All wisdom is within you and will come from there."

I went home after the meeting and started looking for spiritual teachers. There were many of them, and there was a lot of content on the internet. I started listening to each lecture one after the other, following them closely. The next time I met Guðbjörg, she asked me if I had found a spiritual teacher online and what I thought.

"I found a few and listened to a few lectures, but I understood little of what they were saying. I clearly haven't come far enough to understand this," I replied.

Guðbjörg looked at me for a long time and then said, "Everything is not always what it seems. The teaching should be such that everyone understands. Maybe you have a room full of people and you have to give a lecture, and the first thing your spiritual guides do is read the room and find out what is to be discussed, what it is that the people need to hear each and every time. That way you will be a

156

good teacher and lecturer, and those who come to listen to you will understand and accept what is said."

I looked at Guðbjörg and thought, "She is an infinite source of knowledge and wisdom."

When I left Guðbjörg, I thought to myself, "How grateful I am to have found a teacher like Guðbjörg who can help me help others." But at that time I didn't have the courage to tell her this directly. I let my thoughts suffice for the time being.

Rising Consciousness

Now I started to practice channeling with Guðbjörg again. I sat down on the sofa and closed my eyes. "Close your eyes and clear your mind. All external sounds are connected to nature. Don't let them bother you," Guðbjörg said, adding, "Relax your whole body on the sofa. Feel yourself sinking into the sofa. Now draw the energy in through the nose and all the way down into the stomach." I followed her instructions to the letter. I finally started to feel a comfortable and soothing energy over my head. I relaxed a lot with this and made myself comfortable on the couch. There was a long silence, then Guðbjörg asked, "What are you doing now? Are you in no man's land?"

I gave a slight smile. "You might say that," I replied.

"You should not be relaxing now," said Guðbjörg. "You should work and channel to me."

But I sensed no information, and it was as if I had nothing to say and no desire to speak. That's how it went for the entire session. Nothing happened.

The same thing happened for the next few sessions. I didn't understand what I was supposed to do. Guðbjörg tried to guide me in every possible way, but everything seemed closed. I sensed that I was starting to try my master's patience, and I was starting to feel bad and anxious about coming to her. I felt sad that I was not able to channel and that I was constantly disappointing my teacher. "She will eventually reject me. This won't work," I thought to myself. I did all the homework she gave me as conscientiously as I could, and I always agreed to what she asked me to do, but to no avail.

Then I had one of those strong dreams. Guðbjörg's apartment was furnished in such a way that there was one wall separating the kitchen and the living room, and you could enter the kitchen from the living room on both sides of the wall. It was therefore possible to walk in a circle, from the living room into the kitchen and from the kitchen into the living room again on the other side. I dreamed that I was standing in Guðbjörg's living room. I was standing next to the sofa where I was used to sitting and was watching Guðbjörg and me as she sat in the chair and I on the sofa. She was teaching me. She asked me again and again to walk around the kitchen and come back into the living room on the other side. I sat there and always answered, "Yes, I will." But I didn't move, only smiled. Everything seemed stuck. Then, as I stood on the floor looking at us, I heard her say, "You do not accept what is said. You affirm without understanding and accepting." This was a strong message from my guides that I both understood and accepted.

In the next session with Guðbjörg, I told her about the dream, and she listened carefully. She said, "Your dreams, Viktor, are very exciting and interesting. But this is the heart of the matter."

I looked at Guðbjörg and said, "I need to make more of an effort to understand and accept."

She added, "There is a big difference between understanding and accepting. When you accept something, there's no doubt about it. You feel it in your chest. You experience great relief and are impressed. What you accept you do not forget. It sticks and you don't have to look it up later to remember. You can hear something that enters your mind, but it doesn't go any further. A few days later it is gone and forgotten. You accept these strong dreams of yours, and therefore you remember them so well. You will remember them just as clearly in ten, twenty years and beyond."

Guðbjörg looked at me for a long time, and I saw that she had become overshadowed and was about to connect. Finally, she said, "Thoth has come and wants to meet you. He was the priest king of Atlantis and then went to Egypt when Atlantis collapsed. He was the one who built the pyramids. He was the god of wisdom and knowledge in ancient Egypt. I rarely channel him because the energy is so great and it takes a toll on the body to channel. But before him Adam appears, who is a ten-year-old boy, and he will talk to you for a while. Afterward, Thoth will come. I don't know what he wants to say, but he wants to say something."

It was exciting, and I adjusted myself to be more comfortable on the couch. Guðbjörg took off her glasses, closed her eyes, and began to quickly pull air into her nose and breathe out of her mouth for a long time. All of a sudden, she said in a childlike voice, "Hello, I'm Adam."

I returned the greeting as if I were talking to a child, and Adam stood up and pushed the coffee table away. "How are you, Viktor?" he asked.

I smiled. "Everything is fine here with me."

Adam stood in front of me and started drawing the dirty energy from me with his hands. "You really have a lot of rubbish inside of you, Viktor. You're like a dumpster," Adam said, laughing. "There's no reason to live and walk around like that. This just makes you worry and anxious. You need to get rid of the anxiety that is keeping you from helping people. Stop absorbing dirty energy from others and the environment."

I listened carefully to what was said. "Will I help people? Will it work?" I asked with doubt in my words.

"It will happen. God says so, and that is what he wants." Then Adam returned to the chair again and said softly, "I have to go. He's coming."

I eagerly followed everything that happened. This was a new experience for me. I did not know that Guðbjörg was channeling Thoth. "Once again my teacher surprises me," I thought to myself while Guðbjörg connected with Thoth.

Guðbjörg was shaking, and there seemed to be a great conflict taking place in her body. I sensed them as I sat on the couch and watched. Finally, she extended her right hand, which was completely straight, and pointed toward me with two fingers. The hand moved up and down my body. Sometimes the movements were like he was pulling something out. While this was going on, Thoth was buzzing loudly, but he didn't say anything and seemed to be working with the energy in my body. But at last Thoth said in a very deep, raspy voice, "My friend, this helps you forward. We get the energy and flow started in your body."

As soon as he let out the words, he felt more and more, and I got goosebumps all over my body. It was like I was cooling down. "This is having an effect," I thought to myself.

"Do you feel this?" Thoth asked quickly, and I answered with a short yes. "Relax and just accept, my friend," Thoth said.

I suddenly began to involuntarily clench my hands, and then I noticed that Thoth had opened one eye to a small slit and was looking at me sharply. In sharp and determined words, he said, "Let your hands be, boy. Put them down and receive the energy."

I quickly did as he instructed. I felt how much energy was coming from Thoth, and I was speechless. I sat in awe, watching, and I began to sense better and better how the energy and flow had been initiated within me.

After a good while, Thoth said, "That's it, friend. We'll leave it at that for now. We will meet again!"

Guðbjörg calmly came back from the connection and said, "Wow, that was a struggle."

I looked at her. "It was a great experience, and I felt it went well," I replied.

"He wanted to see you specifically," said Guðbjörg. "I have not experienced before that he wants to come and actually asks for it."

I was curious and asked, "Do you think I will connect with him?"

Guðbjörg smiled. "Time will tell. Who knows?"

This was interesting, and I began to feel a difference in the energy in my body after this meeting with Thoth. The energy above my head had started to increase significantly and come to me more often. I also felt that I was lighter on the inside. A few days after the meeting, I started to feel a lot of itching all over my body, but mostly in my legs. I took ever more frequent baths to reduce the itching. I called Guðbjörg and asked what this itch was. She answered, "Your frequency and energy are rising, and it has this effect on the body while it's happening. This is progress, boy, and nothing to fear."

I found all these changes in my mind and body very interesting and exciting—there was always something new happening. Something I had not tried before or experienced. Another thing that I started to experience after the meeting with Thoth was that I sometimes heard a lot of ringing in my ears, and it alternated between the right and left ear. It was extremely rare for me to hear this in both ears at the same time. The duration varied but was usually short. I told Guðbjörg about this in the next class, and she explained to me that it was them sending me messages and information from the other side. "Suddenly you know a lot of things you didn't know before," Guðbjörg said.

I thought about this for a long time and then said, "There is a lot to learn and a lot of changes happening in my body and mind. This is very exciting and at the same time fun to observe."

Guðbjörg answered, "Very much so." She repeated herself with emphasis: "Very much so." Then she added, "But you're just getting started. You must change more still, friend. We are just starting to work with you."

I left Guðbjörg happy and satisfied after this meeting. I felt that I had experienced great progress and change after the meeting with Thoth. I drove home to Kistufell and went for a long walk. The weather was beautiful and clear, but it was cold. I reflected on what had happened and thanked my spiritual guides, Thoth and Guðbjörg, for their help and the success I had achieved.

Guðbjörg held a course at her home called Opening to Mediumship and invited me to come. "You will connect with your spiritual guides," she said as she invited me to the course. I came full of anticipation and arrived at Guðbjörg's on time. There were twelve of us doing the course. Guðbjörg first talked to us and then had us meditate to calm our minds and to get us to arrive, as she called it—to bring the mind away from the hustle and bustle of everyday life. Then we were split into groups of two. There was a woman who was also a beginner who started channeling to me. She encouraged me in what I was doing and seemed to have a good way of channeling. Much of what she channeled was correct, and I was able to say, "Yes, that's right. Yes, that fits," when it was relevant to encourage her and to help her.

"Let's switch," Guðbjörg called out to the group. I changed chairs with the woman and started to calm my mind and relax. But I saw nothing and had nothing to say, and after a long silence, Guðbjörg came to us and calmly put her hand on my shoulder. "How's it going?"

I cleared my throat. "I'm energized, but I don't have anything to say," I answered hopelessly.

"Just start talking to this beautiful and lovely woman. Feel in your heart that you want to help her. Where is the desire and the spark?" Then Guðbjörg started helping the next students.

I started talking to the woman and telling her the first thing that came to mind. But I sensed that this was not deep and sincere channeling. The first part of the course ended at midnight on Friday, and we then met again on Saturday morning at ten, with the course lasting until two. I had a really hard time falling asleep when I got home on Friday night and felt a lot of energy inside me. But I finally fell asleep and woke up very tired, feeling like I hadn't slept in a week. When we met again at Guðbjörg's place, she started asking each of us how we were doing and how we had slept. I told her that I had trouble sleeping and was very tired. She smiled. "This is progress, my friend. These are changes in the energy, and there is a great cleansing taking place." We continued to practice channeling until the course concluded around two. I was grateful that there were changes and improvements in the energy within me, but at the same time, I felt disappointed in my channeling performance.

During this time, I often thought and said to my guides things like "If I get a connection with you, this and that will happen." I later learned that doubt in thoughts and words diminishes and hinders success in what is being done. It is not good to be full of doubts when embarking on new projects and subjects.

There were two of us at the branch of the engineering office in Akranes, and I mostly sat alone in my private office, my colleague in the next room. There was a shared kitchenette with a large kitchen table that also served as a meeting facility. This was exactly what I needed at the time, privacy and a quiet work environment. But there was a lot to do and a lot of pressure, and I had started to learn not to let it disturb my peace. I prioritized my tasks, and then I worked on one task at a time in peace and balance. My performance increased this way. "I have learned this from Guðbjörg," I thought to myself. While working on a project, I used to stress over the next one. "I can only work on one thing at a time, and I do it best in peace and balance," I thought to myself. There was a beautiful view of the mountains outside the office window, and Akrafjall and Skarðsheiði were in full view. I listened a lot to Mozart and other classical music when I had the chance at work. I felt how it calmed me down and helped me reach an inner balance. On the weekday that I had an appointment with Guðbjörg, I worked at the company's headquarters in Reykjavík. I left work for a little over an hour, usually just after noon. At the headquarters it was a completely different environment, because there I sat in an open space surrounded by other employees, and there was therefore much more ambient noise and interaction. Little by little, I learned not to let this disturb my peace either.

One day I had an appointment with Guðbjörg, so I drove to the headquarters in Reykjavík. I felt like I hadn't been to see her for weeks, even though I saw her every week. When I had settled down on the sofa, I said to Guðbjörg, "Can I tell you something?"

She smiled. "Please do, go ahead."

I adjusted myself on the sofa and said, "Now I am working in a quiet environment in Akranes with my own office, and there are only two of us in the office. There are few distractions there. Every now and then I work in Reykjavík, where there are a lot of people and many distractions. I'm starting to feel that it no longer matters to me where I am—I'm still calm and in balance. This is a new experience for me. Before, I got excited because there were a lot of people around and a lot of stimuli."

Spiritual Awakening

Guðbjörg smiled broadly. "I'm happy to hear this because it means you're making progress. One of the things we teach is communication with other people. Not letting others control your feelings and well-being. For example, even if there is a person speaking loudly to you and has a lot going on, you keep your calm and balance. Some people let others create anger, hatred, and fear within them, and thus others are the ones who control how they feel. You learn to be calm and balanced in different situations and with different people.

"You will also learn to shield yourself against other people's thoughts. For example, if a person thinks badly of you, you may start to feel bad but have no idea why. Ask God our creator for protection and blessings. Don't let others control how you feel. I hear you are well on your way with this. Continue on this path and you will learn to be calm and balanced in all situations and with all different people. This applies equally to joy and success as well as hardship and adversity. You are experiencing a freedom you have never experienced before. Continue on this path, my friend," Guðbjörg finished with a smile.

The energy was starting to come over me more often. I thought it was wonderful because I gained a lot of calm and balance and my anxiety disappeared during these moments.

A day before I was supposed to have another session with her, Guðbjörg called me. "Viktor, I wanted to see if you would be interested in channeling to one of my students tomorrow. She has booked a session just before you and is ready to sit for longer so you can practice channeling."

Although I got a knot of anxiety in my stomach, I immediately answered, "Yes, I am. That's exciting." I knew that I had to develop my courage and self-confidence if I intended to help people in this way in the future.

I had a lot of anxiety and felt uncomfortable when I drove to Guðbjörg. I thought to myself, "I need to get rid of this anxiety that has plagued me for many years." I had arrived at Guðbjörg's, and I saw how my finger trembled when I rang the doorbell.

"Come on in, Viktor," I heard over the intercom, and I walked in and ascended the stairs. The door was open when I reached the landing, and I entered. I heard Guðbjörg talking to someone in the living room, and she called to me, "Just come on in. We are here in the living room."

I took off my jacket and my shoes and slowly walked down the hall. I saw Guðbjörg in her chair, and across from her was a young woman sitting on the couch. Guðbjörg said, "This is Viktor, my student who is going to make a difference and help people by channeling information and education to them. He needs more practice in channeling. Viktor, this is your fellow student who has been with me before and has come back to continue. She is ready to help you practice channeling."

I walked over to the sofa and held out my hand. "Hi," I said. "I'm Viktor." The woman got up and took my hand

and said hello. Then I walked over to Guðbjörg and said, "Shouldn't we greet each other properly?" I opened my arms, and Guðbjörg stood up and we hugged warmly.

"Of course we should," Guðbjörg said, adding, "It's good to get grounded from you, my friend." I tried to behave well even though there was a lot of tension and anxiety inside me. Guðbjörg pointed to her chair and said, "Now you should sit here, dear Viktor. The woman and I will sit here on the couch and you will channel." We went to our seats, and then Guðbjörg said, "Well, Viktor, now get comfortable in the chair and relax. Take a deep breath and calm your mind. Breathe all the way into your stomach and out slowly." I did everything as Guðbjörg instructed, and after a while she said, "Ask your Father who is in heaven to help you do good for this woman. Now put your mind on her and channel to her with your feelings. That is where the channeling comes from, not from your head or your thoughts." I did this, but there seemed to be no information coming, and I started to get agitated because I wasn't doing well in this task.

After a long silence, Guðbjörg said, "You need to forget yourself. The only thing that matters is to do good for the woman sitting here." Time passed, and not much was happening, but finally Guðbjörg said to the woman, "Now you should ask the boy about something you want to know."

She quickly asked, "Do you see my children?"

171

Before she had finished speaking, I saw three girls who all looked different ages because of their size. "I see three girls who all seem to have been born in different years—the size I see here indicates that—and they all have blonde hair."

The woman replied, "That's right. That's correct."

Guðbjörg agreed. "This is absolutely correct. Keep going."

I continued to describe the girls and what they would do in the future. The information flowed out of me automatically without any thought, and I felt how easy it was. I visualized images, which I then described to the woman, and judging by her reaction, it seemed to be correct.

After a good while, Guðbjörg said, "That's enough. Let's not exhaust him." I looked at the clock and saw that I had been channeling for about forty-five minutes.

"Forty-five minutes," I said. "It felt like five."

Guðbjörg replied, "You achieved a deep connection, and then you sense the passing of time. You did very well, boy. This is your best channel yet. First you talked about what is and what has been, and thus you proved yourself as a medium, and then you continued and talked about what is yet to come. This is proof channeling. What did you think, dear? How do you think he performed?"

Spiritual Awakening

The woman smiled. "Very well, everything he said about the past and present fit perfectly, and our future is exciting."

The session was coming to an end. We all got up, and Guðbjörg repeated, "You did well, great progress." I was happy in my heart to hear this, and I said goodbye to the woman with a handshake and embraced Guðbjörg. I was ecstatic as I drove back to work. I had managed to channel—I had managed to forget myself. Times like these at Guðbjörg's were a great motivation and inspiration for me to continue the journey.

When I got home to Kistufell, I decided to take a walk around the area. I dressed warmly and went out into the wind. I started talking to my spiritual guides. I asked them for help to connect with them better and get information from them to pass on to others, to help people and to educate them. I sat by the stream where I had sat many times meditating and practicing emptying my mind. But now I started to put my mind into the future. I imagined the spiritual center Halldóra and I had, and pictured many people staying with us for several days at a time. I was teaching people and helping them. I felt great joy in my heart at these thoughts. "Help is needed in many places," I thought to myself as I looked at the city that lay there in the distance. Then I realized that the weather had stopped bothering me, no longer affecting my well-being like before. Whether it was sunny and warm or windy and raining, I always felt good. "This is a change. It is progress," I thought to myself.

There were great changes taking place within me, both conscious and unconscious. My mindset was changing a lot. I had become positive and remained calm and in balance in different situations. These changes happened slowly. However, I still felt anxiety and fear every now and then. During this time, my main goal with Guðbjörg's classes was to connect with my spiritual guides in order to be able to share knowledge and information. But really, the purpose of the sessions was to help me on the spiritual path to find myself, my true self.

A few days later the phone rang. "Hello," Guðbjörg said, and I became happier at her voice.

"Hi," I replied.

She added, "You have an appointment with me tomorrow, and Thoth wants to see you again."

I was excited by the news. "I'm looking forward to it," I responded, adding, "Thoth had a big impact on me last time he came, and it will be exciting to see what happens now."

Guðbjörg replied, "Absolutely. I'm also looking forward to seeing what will happen. I look forward to seeing you," Guðbjörg added, and we said goodbye.

I was wondering for a long time what would happen. "How do I connect with Thoth? Why does he want to help me of all people?" I thought to myself.

Full of anticipation, I drove to Guðbjörg the next day. I walked in and she greeted me. "Welcome, dear friend," she said as she embraced me. "You are coming for an operation," Guðbjörg said as soon as we entered the living room.

"Operation?" I answered quickly in surprise.

We took our seats and Guðbjörg added, "Yes, Thoth is going to open your throat chakra to get the speech going and to strengthen your voice." She looked at me for a long time. "What do you think?"

I almost couldn't comprehend what was happening, but I answered without thinking more about it. "Sounds good. It's good to get help from Thoth."

Guðbjörg took off her glasses and clearly intended to start right away. "Take off your glasses and get comfortable on the sofa. Unbutton the top three buttons on your shirt so that it airs well around your neck."

I followed all of Guðbjörg's instructions. She had started to connect, and soon Adam arrived and was as light spirited as before. He spoke to me briefly and then said, "I have to go—HE is coming." I thanked him, and then a great struggle started in Guðbjörg's body. She rumbled, and soon she had connected. Thoth had arrived in the living room.

"Hello," a deep, husky voice said. "Now I'm going to open the throat chakra." Thoth got up and walked slowly toward me. "Lift your chin up, my friend, and close your eyes." I felt a gust of wind around my neck, and I felt Thoth swinging his hand close by my neck. After a short while, Thoth said, "Now it'll feel like a stab in the neck." Without him touching me, I felt a sharp pain. It was like getting stabbed with a pin or a knife in the throat. "All is as it should be," Thoth said in his deep voice. "So it shall be," he added. He continued on my neck for a bit and then said, "It's done. Good luck, friend." My throat now felt sore, as if I were sick.

I sat there motionless with my eyes closed for a good while, then heard Guðbjörg ask, "Well, friend, how do you feel?" I opened my eyes, put on my glasses, and described to Guðbjörg the pain in my neck and what a strange and remarkable experience this was. Guðbjörg stood up and, as she passed me on her way into the kitchen, said, "I'm going to prepare a drink for you to soothe your throat." I heard her moving around the kitchen, and she returned shortly with warm orange juice. "Here you go," she told me. "It'll help your throat." I took the glass, thanked her, and started drinking. "You'll feel this for two days," Guðbjörg said, taking a seat in the chair across from me. "He is powerful, Thoth," she said and sighed.

"It was an indescribable experience," I replied, adding, "Now I have sensed the connection between the spiritual and the physical. It's not as far apart as one might think. Strange how spiritual things can affect us physically in a direct way. The experience was as if someone was doing an operation on me with their hands—remarkable."

Guðbjörg smiled and said, "This was an amazing time."

I rebuttoned my shirt. "This was a great and remarkable experience," I added. I stood up and said goodbye to Guðbjörg with a hug.

"Let me observe you, my friend," she said.

I hugged her tightly and replied, "Sure."

I walked down the stairs and got into the car. I sat in the car for a long time before starting it. "What an experience that was," I thought to myself. I sat there for a long time thinking about it all before I drove off to work. It was difficult to concentrate on work after this session. I felt a pain in my neck that lasted for about two days, just as Thoth and Guðbjörg had told me. A few days later, I felt the energy that had previously only been above my head now reaching down to my neck. I also felt more energy coming over me as it reached further down. My voice had become stronger, firmer, and more determined. This was great progress, for which I was grateful.

Guðbjörg continued to help me so that I could channel my spiritual guides in a trance, but it did not go well. I managed to get the energy down to my throat, but I was always in no man's land and had nothing to say and no pictures in my mind to describe.

"When you channel from the higher planes, you don't see any pictures. The speech gets going and flows directly through you. All you have to do is move to the side for the time being for them to get space. When you channel from the lower realms, you see images that you can describe to the person who is with you. It's different here," Guðbjörg explained.

"I don't know how I can step aside in the meantime," I answered.

Guðbjörg smiled. "You are so curious and want to observe." Then she added, "Imagine you are in your favorite place in your house. Then you will forget yourself and give them the stage."

I was bad at this, and it took many hours to practice and master it. I managed to draw in the energy but never managed to speak—it felt like I was the one doing the talking.

"When I did this for the first time, I thought, 'This won't kill me,' and I let myself go and everything got going," Guðbjörg recounted, doing her best to help me continue.

I was losing hope that this would work, and one time when I was driving to Guðbjörg for my regular session, I was determined to stop. I was going to thank her for all the help and tell her I was done. When I got to her place and we took a seat in the living room, with her sitting there in the chair across from me smiling, and we started talking about this and that, a great calm and peace came over me. I felt a great desire to continue, and I quickly forgot what I had intended to tell her.

Sometimes I would go a long time without noticing any changes, then all of a sudden there would be huge changes and lots of progress in one fell swoop. If the saying good things happen slowly ever applies, it is in regard to spiritual awakening and opening. Once, Guðbjörg, when I was getting impatient, said to me, "Your frequency and energy are increasing, and this has to happen slowly so that your body doesn't short circuit."

Although I had a hard time connecting with and channeling my spiritual guides, many things were changing in my life. In the past, the opinions of others about what I was doing mattered a lot to me. Up until then, I had been living based on other people's expectations or what I thought their expectations were. I suddenly realized that these no longer mattered to me. I was taking a walk outside Kistufell when I felt these constraints had left me. "I am free from other people's opinions about what I am doing in my life," I thought to myself. "What a relief. I am whole and honest toward others. That is what matters."

I felt how the shackles of my mind were being released one by one. Now I was beginning to prioritize well-being. I told Guðbjörg what I had realized and that up until now I had been a prisoner of others' opinions of me and my life. Guðbjörg smiled. "I'm pleased to hear and see how your consciousness is rising. You are gaining more and more freedom from others." I agreed, and she added, "Look what a great illusion everything is and how much we deceived ourselves and were prisoners of our minds and thoughts. All this was a mindset, something that only existed in the mind."

I agreed with every word. "Exactly right," I said.

Ragnar Viktor Karlsson

Guðbjörg continued, "As you know, we are different, and each of our tasks is different. The souls have different roles, and the ages of the souls are different. The life tasks are different for each soul. For example, look at your journey. Many people around you do not understand what you are doing or where you are going and therefore cannot judge you and your actions. In the same way, we must not judge others for their actions, but support each person on their journey.

"When you raise your consciousness, as you are doing now, you gain an overview of life and existence and the people around you. You begin to understand each person's journey and path and realize where the person is in their journey. You gain this deep understanding of people and life in general. This is one of your tools for the future when you start teaching and helping people. You know exactly where the person is and what they need."

I felt great anticipation inside me while Guðbjörg spoke. I looked forward to helping people and guiding them.

Guðbjörg continued, "He who judges will be judged. This is what we have discussed today."

I answered quickly: "Precisely." There was a long silence as I fell into thought, and then I said, "One of the biggest aspects of our lives can be said to be communication with others in one way or another. The task is to learn this communication and become free from other people, to not let others disturb our peace and well-being, to always be in balance in this communication."

Guðbjörg smiled broadly. "You have understood and accepted this, and I am happy to hear that. This is great progress." Her words made my heart happy. She added, "Communication comes with emotions, and those are the ones we are experiencing here on Earth as we are learning little by little to control them. It is important to always be aware of how you are feeling. If you find that there is someone who has started to have a negative effect on your well-being, you can take control immediately and avoid this instead of letting it grow inside you."

I answered thoughtfully, "How strange life and existence are."

Guðbjörg looked at me for a long time and then said, "You could say that." She added, "As you've noticed, the changes in us happen slowly. Sometimes we change without knowing. At times, you are teaching a person something that you have gone through and experienced before, and the person sits and listens but neither understands nor accepts what you are saying. Then, much later, she can begin to understand and accept what you said. Never let yourself react to this. We all need a different amount of time to understand and accept things. But you sow seeds in people that later become beautiful flowers. Therefore, you need to be tolerant and patient with your future students. Do you understand?"

Ragnar Viktor Karlsson

I sat there on the sofa, thinking, "It's strange how the sessions with Guðbjörg are different. Sometimes I'm learning to connect with my spiritual guides and to channel, and then I'm learning about myself, to raise my consciousness and frequency to develop further and to make myself feel better inside and become freer from others. This is so completely different."

After a long silence, Guðbjörg asked, "What are you thinking about?" I smiled and told Guðbjörg about my thoughts, and she answered right away, "This is not so different. You are dealing with yourself and your false self, so you raise your consciousness and thus manage to connect with your guides. The higher your consciousness, the higher you reach in channeling."

Now I started to understand how it all connected. I now saw that Guðbjörg's teaching was concise and led me forward step by step into a higher consciousness and frequency and thus enabled me to channel the high planes. In the beginning, I thought it was just about mastering the technique of channeling, ensuring the energy I drew in to channel was aligned with my consciousness. Up until that point, I had put the greatest emphasis on achieving a connection with my spiritual guides, because at the beginning that was my only goal in studying with Guðbjörg.

There was a long silence again, then Guðbjörg said in a firm voice, "Let's continue on this path. I'm going to give you a big homework assignment."

I interjected, "I'm up for it."

She continued, "It's forgiveness. First of all, you need to forgive yourself, then you need to ask forgiveness from others for your wrongdoings, and finally you need to forgive those who have wronged you in life. This is a difficult task and can take time. Some avoid facing this task and procrastinate. Be brave and strong and it will work out. Ask your Heavenly Father, God your creator, to help you in this task—and be sincere.

"When you forgive others, get comfortable in a chair or lie down and imagine that the person you are going to forgive is standing or sitting in front of you. Then you say to him in your mind, 'I feel that you have wronged me in some way in the past, and I am now going to forgive you from the bottom of my heart.' You need to put your mind inside your chest and do this with your feelings, not with your head. This is how this is achieved. Then, the next day, do the same as before and close your eyes and imagine that the same person has come in front of you, and now see what feelings come up in your chest—is it hate or anger or pure love? When you experience unconditional love for the person, you have forgiven them, but not before.

"This may take time and many attempts. If you fail, it's because you haven't done it with your heart, but with your head. As soon as you do this with your heart sincerely, it's done. Some may say, 'How can you expect me to forgive this person? Do you know what she has done to me over the years?' Regardless of how bad or difficult the person has been, we must be able to forgive in order to be free.

Thus do we gain freedom and settle all obligations to the person. Because of such considerations, many fail in this task or put it off. But you will experience even more freedom if you do this—that's guaranteed," Guðbjörg finally concluded, looking at me sharply.

After a short while, I answered, "I'll do this."

The session came to an end. We got up, and as we walked to the lobby, I said, "Once again you have filled me with wisdom for my benefit."

Guðbjörg patted me on the shoulder and said, "It's good that you're happy, friend." I said goodbye with a warm hug. "Bye for now," she called after me down the stairs.

Internal Cleansing

Recently, I had been focusing on myself and my spiritual opening and could therefore not build or give much thought to our spiritual center at Kistufell. The number of visitors had steadily decreased. As a result, Halldóra and I began to think about whether we should move back home to our apartment in Krummahólar. Around the same time, we received a letter from the owners of Kistufell saying that they wanted to raise the rent significantly. They had thus made our decision easy. We decided to move, and within a few weeks we moved back to Krummahólar.

We prepared a "spiritual" room where I could meditate and achieve inner peace. I started walking around Elliðaárdalur again, on the paths, in the forest, and along the river. "This is paradise on Earth," I often thought to myself as I enjoyed the nature in the valley. I also started visiting the neighborhood pool again. It was nice to let the fatigue slip out of my body in the hot tubs. "It is a privilege to have this hot water here in Iceland," I said to myself more than once.

Our time at Kistufell was a great adventure, and we met a lot of people who started coming to us regularly. Now this chapter was over and new adventures were about to begin.

The forgiveness that was my homework assignment was threefold in my mind. First of all, I had to forgive myself. Then, I had to ask for forgiveness for my wrongdoings toward others. Finally, I had to forgive those who had wronged me. For the first time in my spiritual journey, I began to ask God for help. Until then, I had talked to my spiritual guides and asked them for help and inspiration. Now this started to change.

"Heavenly Father—God, my creator, help me, and show me the right way."

I remembered that forgiveness is a big part of the Lord's prayer that I had said so often. "Forgive us our debts, as we forgive our debtors."

"The debts are my misdeeds in life toward others," I thought to myself, and I decided to start with that part. I went into the room and settled down in a comfortable chair. I closed my eyes and began to recall my life from childhood to the present day. Then I started to remember incidents that I wished I could take back and have undone. There were many incidents that arose from my school years, instances involving my fellow students and the school's staff and teachers. I had been unfair at times, and my teasing went too far. As I started to recall these things, I realized that I had very likely hurt the person in question with my words and behavior. I had used ugly and hurtful words. I had always avoided all physical violence, but my words could be sharp and difficult to deal with. It was hard and shocking to recall all of this, and I felt very guilty and began to regret my actions. I felt sadness in my heart. That was very difficult.

"Heavenly Father—God, my creator, I repent of my wrongdoings and ask for forgiveness."

I imagined that the person from each of the incidents that came to my mind was standing in front of me, and I spoke to them from the heart. "I know that I have done you wrong in the past. I repent and ask for forgiveness." Thus I went through my entire childhood and my life until the present day. Some incidents involved relatives, friends, coworkers, and other people I had met. Some of them I had met only once. The hardest part was going through this process with my closest relatives, my friends, and my wife Halldóra. It took many days, but I went through it with as much sincerity as I could. This was one of the homework assignments that I couldn't finish in one week. The first part took many weeks, and for a long time afterward I recalled incidents from the past for which I repented and asked for forgiveness. I felt relieved, and I started to feel progressively better. During my walks, I used to review my life and my relationships. In this way I recalled more incidents. I went over everything carefully to make sure I forgot no one, and I took my time with this part.

Finally, I thought to myself, "Now I have settled my debts, and now I have to go over my debtors." Now I had to forgive those who had wronged me in life. It was all the more difficult and also took a long time. At first I thought to myself, "Some things cannot be forgiven. How can I possibly do that?" I had already understood and accepted that this was necessary to do in order to move forward on my spiritual path and gain freedom.

In the same way as before, I sat down in a chair in the spiritual room and closed my eyes and began to recall my life from childhood to the present day. There really weren't many people who came to mind who had done me wrong in my life, but there were a few. I decided to work on two the first night. As before, I put my mind inside to my heart and used my feelings and heart to forgive. I imagined that the person in question was sitting in front of me, and I looked at him for a long time. I felt my chest fill with anger and hatred, but I said aloud, "In my mind you have done me wrong in the past, and I will hereby forgive you from the bottom of my heart." Then I imagined the person getting up and walking away.

The next day I sat back in the chair and closed my eyes and imagined that the same person was now sitting in front of me again, and I looked at her for a long time and began to feel the feelings that rose in my chest. I felt hatred and anger again. "I haven't forgiven yet," I thought to myself, and I went through the forgiveness process again in the same way as before. After going through this process countless times, I finally sat down to do the same as before. The person in question was once again sitting in front of me, and I began to notice the feelings in my chest. Finally, I felt a lot of love in my heart for that person. All the anger and hatred were gone, and I felt a lot of relief. I felt so much love and so much relief that I was convinced that the forgiveness had succeeded. "It worked," I thought to myself happily and gratefully. This took a long time and tested my patience. I had almost given up hope that this would work, but it did. I went through this process with all my "debtors," and like before it took me many attempts to be able to forgive.

In the end, I had to forgive myself, accept the past, and put it behind me. I began to recall all the mistakes I had made in life and the wrong decisions I felt I had made. It took me a long time to come to terms with the past and my actions that affected only myself. I asked God, my creator, to help me and guide me in this process. I sat down and closed my eyes and imagined myself standing in front of me. I looked at myself and said, "I forgive myself for my wrongdoings against myself. I have hereby come to terms with my past." I did this many times until I felt that a heavy burden was lifted from me, and I felt that the wrongdoings of the past no longer disturbed my peace. I now saw them as experiences and lessons.

This process of forgiveness was extremely demanding and took a long time. For me, this was one of the hardest things I had gone through in my spiritual opening.

I felt a great relief after the forgiveness process, as if a very heavy burden had been lifted from me. I experienced much more freedom than before. Having gone through this process, I fully understood why so many people procrastinate and avoid dealing with forgiveness. But there will always be days of guilt—everyone will eventually face their actions toward themselves and others and have to experience in their own chest the feelings they have created

---

for others with their actions and words. Now that I had gone through this, I had a great desire to teach others to do the same.

Guðbjörg had followed me closely during the forgiveness process, and I informed her about my progress every week. Finally, after many weeks, I told Guðbjörg, "Now I think I have finished this homework assignment. It was much more difficult and shocking than I imagined when I started."

Guðbjörg smiled. "You did well, boy. I am proud of you now."

It gladdened my heart to hear my teacher pleased with my performance. "It was a difficult task," I said. Then I added, "There were some people I had a hard time forgiving at first, but then I got the hang of it and followed your advice and went through the process. I thought a lot about this on walks and strengthened myself in this undertaking."

Guðbjörg listened attentively and said, "You did the right thing. Do you feel relieved after this?"

I gave it some thought and said, "There is a big difference. I also felt it every time I was able to forgive from the heart. It was as if a slab had been lifted off my chest and I felt a great sense of relief. It was clear when I achieved this. But I had to exercise a lot of patience and be brave to make it happen."

Guðbjörg carefully followed what I said and replied, "This is a big conflict, dealing with yourself and sorting yourself out. You don't get anything on a silver platter here, and there are no shortcuts."

I understood this and said, "The saying good things happen slowly is very fitting here." Guðbjörg agreed.

There was a long silence, but finally Guðbjörg said, "Now contact your spiritual guides and let me talk to them. Don't you think it's about time?"

I immediately felt slight anxiety on hearing these words, but I answered, "Yes, of course." I took off my glasses, closed my eyes, and started to relax on the couch. Finally, I felt energy coming down my head and my neck.

"Yes, you're doing this correctly," Guðbjörg said.

Then I started smiling, happiness coming over me.

"He has come through. I can see it in your face. Keep drawing in the energy." A few minutes passed. "Hello and welcome," Guðbjörg said.

I replied, "Hello there."

Guðbjörg continued to guide me. "Keep talking so the flow will start. Who are you?" Guðbjörg asked.

I answered the first thing that came to mind: "We are the Tibetan monks, and we are here to help the boy get started."

Guðbjörg cheerfully answered, "Welcome. How are you?"

191

Ragnar Viktor Karlsson

I received more energy and continued, "We were with the boy in a Tibetan monastery around 1500. There the boy was a spiritual guru. It was a comfortable life, as we could focus on ourselves, our spiritual development, and the work in the monastery. Nevertheless, it was still physically demanding because the monastery was built into a mountainside, and there was a steep path down to the fields. We had to carry everything up that steep gravel path." While I was channeling, it was in the monastery. I could see all of it.

"Anything else?" Guðbjörg asked after a short silence. "Keep talking to maintain the connection."

I cleared my throat and continued. "We were busy in the monastery all day. The days were long, and we had many tasks. We grew all our food ourselves and were self-sufficient. Then there were meditations and prayer sessions at regular intervals. The monastery has a large collection of information on spiritual matters. All the text is on scrolls and is kept in a library. There are guides on spiritual matters, the history of mankind, the stars, and much more. This is a lot of knowledge and information that is fun to look at and dig through. Unfortunately, the spiritual part of man has given way to the worldly part. All of this has to be in balance so that the person feels good. This has always been true at all times. Nothing changes within us, even though our environment and technology change. Many have grown distant to themselves."

Guðbjörg asked a question: "Was the Dalai Lama there with you?"

192

I answered, "No, he wasn't with us, but he was in the capital Lhasa. When we were there, it was the second Dalai Lama who was the spiritual leader of Tibet. We rarely went to the capital, as it took very long, and traveling over a mountain range was a long and demanding journey."

In the end, Guðbjörg said, "That's enough. Let's not exhaust the boy."

A smile came to my lips. "We thank you dearly for the time we spent together today, and we'll hear from you again soon," the monks said to Guðbjörg.

I felt the energy leave my body. It felt like I had fallen asleep and was waking up. I slowly opened my eyes and started rubbing them. I finally put on my glasses and looked at Guðbjörg, who sat in her chair and smiled happily. "I was channeling," I said with joy in my heart.

"That's right," Guðbjörg said. Then she added, "Congratulations, boy. You did well. We will continue next time."

Our time was up, and I said goodbye to Guðbjörg with a warm hug.

I was happy and satisfied in my heart while I drove away from Guðbjörg. "I was able to channel," I thought to myself. "It worked." I remembered the year mentioned in the channeling and the second Dalai Lama. I was excited to find out whether this was correct. Did the second Dalai Lama the live around 1500? I looked it up in a hurry when I got to work, and I read online: the second Dalai Lama—

born 1475 and died 1542. I was happy. "It was correct," I thought to myself. I could channel.

But this joy was short lived, because in the next session I could not utter a word and was unable to channel anything. I did everything as before, but to no avail. This was a huge setback—and in my opinion a step backward. The next sessions with Guðbjörg went similarly. I couldn't channel at all, and everything was stuck. Strong thoughts started coming to my mind to abort this journey, that I didn't have it in me. "A king and a scholar are too earthly of soul roles to be able to channel. It is only the priests and the artists who have the talent to do this," I thought. I went for long walks, and as I started to feel down, I almost convinced myself to give up. Thus several days passed in despair and resignation.

One day after work, I went for a long walk through Elliðaárdalur Valley. I was walking alone on a narrow forest path when suddenly and without thinking I said aloud, "Jesus Christ, leader of my life and my savior, I have forgotten you in all that I have been through recently. Forgive me, my dear friend, and I ask for your guidance and blessing on my spiritual journey." I repeatedly called out, "Help me, my dear friend and savior."

A few days later, I woke up and got ready to go to work. I had decided to work at the office in Reykjavík that day. I usually arrived at work at seven in the morning, so I sat alone for about an hour in the large open space in the office before my coworkers came to work at eight. I turned on the computer and stared at the screen but couldn't get to work. I was thinking about how I should inform Guðbjörg that I would stop this process and abort the journey. I couldn't continue.

I sat almost motionless at the desk when I felt that someone put their hand on my left shoulder. I was not startled but sat there calmly and began to wonder what it was. Then I heard a man say, "Be patient and brave, my dear friend. I am always with you. I will answer your call. You will be a spiritual teacher like I was. I had to go through the same thing you are going through now before I started teaching and making a difference here on Earth. You will succeed, my dear friend. Keep going and your wishes will come true." As I listened to each word, I felt my heart fill with love. I got goosebumps all over my body and felt a chill from head to toe. I sensed great ecstasy and energy throughout my body. When the man had finished speaking, I calmly looked up at him and saw Jesus Christ standing there in a white robe. This was precisely the man who had come to me in a dream some time before, the one who sat on the rock on the hill teaching humanity. He had said to me, "Now it's your turn." Even more goosebumps rose on my skin, and I got even colder. I could feel the love in my heart grow. Finally, Jesus disappeared. My eyes glistened. I had never experienced such love before.

I burst into tears in the office and rushed into the nearest restroom. I sat there and cried relentlessly for about half an hour. "How could they put such a man who carries so much love with him to death?" I thought to myself as I imagined the Crucifixion. After a long time, I got up and looked in the mirror. Tears still streamed down my face. I saw that my eyes and face were swollen from the crying. I heard people coming into the office. So I washed my face and went to my desk. In fact, I didn't fully realize what had happened until the next day, and only then did I begin to accept what had happened. I thought to myself, "I no longer simply believe in Jesus Christ. I have experienced him and his love in my heart."

There was great anticipation inside me when I drove to Guðbjörg for the next session. I looked forward to telling her about what I had experienced. I hurried up the stairs and went in to see her. I greeted her with a warm hug and then said, "I have to tell you something."

She looked at me and replied, "I'm excited. Let's have some coffee and then go into the living room."

I had barely sat down when I began to tell her in detail what I had experienced a few days before. I described how strong the experience and great the love had been.

Guðbjörg stared at me while I recounted the story, and then, after a long silence, she said, "I'm glad to hear it, but it doesn't surprise me. Hold on to his energy." I had expected Guðbjörg to be very surprised by the story, but it was as if she expected such a thing and was not surprised at all. There was a long silence, and then Guðbjörg asked, "But how does Viktor feel?"

I did not understand what she meant, so I asked her, "After this experience?"

She shook her head. "No, I mean in general. Have you changed since you started working with us?"

I finished my coffee before answering. "I feel completely different. It can hardly be described in words. I feel very free from other people. They no longer disturb my peace. I am free from other people's opinions. In the past, it mattered a lot to me what other people thought about what I was doing. That's no longer the case. I have become carefree and live in the moment. I enjoy every moment of my life, whether it is in play or work. I don't think about the future and have stopped dwelling on the past. Everything is balanced. It is as if the problems have disappeared from my life."

Guðbjörg interjected, "That's wonderful to hear. Isn't it a big difference to live like this?"

I looked at her. "It's hard to describe the difference," I answered.

"It's going to get even better," Guðbjörg said, smiling. Then she added, "You have a lot of work to do, but then you will feel better and better."

Without thinking, I said, "But the anxiety is still bothering me. I can feel it, and it makes me sick to my stomach."

Guðbjörg listened attentively. "We need to rid you of the anxiety. When do you want to get rid of it?" she asked with a smile.

"As soon as possible," I replied.

"Anxiety is like an uninvited guest that comes to visit you from time to time," Guðbjörg explained. "It is one manifestation of fear, and it prevents us from experiencing the love in our heart. There is only room for one feeling at a time in our hearts. So choose carefully which feeling to have. You need to learn to be aware of your thoughts, because they control how you feel and they lead to words and actions. That's why you should always be aware of your thoughts. They are as influential as your words and deeds. You can help a person who is far away from you with positive and loving thoughts. Your environment and life are a product of your thoughts. So be aware if a thought starts to arise that will eventually lead to anxiety. Push it away and say, 'No, thank you. You're not welcome here.' At night, you can review what thoughts have gone through your mind that day. Always think positively and lovingly about yourself and others. Then you will feel good, and the fear and anxiety will gradually disappear from your life."

I listened attentively, taking in every word that Guðbjörg said. Then she added, "Then ask your ever-present Father to help you and guide you. You can do that every morning on your way to work. Remember to thank him for his help. This is your homework, boy," Guðbjörg added with a smile. Then she concluded, "It's to be aware of yourself and your thoughts."

I felt happy, because I knew that now I would get the anxiety under control. I knew that the advice and instructions I received from Guðbjörg would work and help me. I just needed to understand, accept, and follow what she said. Then I would feel better and have a higher consciousness. After a long silence, I said, "At school, I gained knowledge and skills, but with you I am gaining wisdom of life."

Guðbjörg smiled and replied, "I'm pleased with you, boy. You are doing well, and you are a very conscientious student." When I stood up and started walking to the lobby, she said, "There is a woman who comes to see me once a week. I suggest you start meeting at her house or at your house and start practicing channeling and healing. You can help each other. How does that sound?"

I didn't take long to think about it, answering, "That is a good idea. I'm up for it."

Guðbjörg patted me on the shoulder and said, "I'll talk to her and ask if she's up for it as well. She channels Yogananda."

I thought about this. "I know her," I realized. "She came to Kistufell and gave me the book on Yogananda. This sounds great." Then I said goodbye to Guðbjörg and thanked her for a good session.

I hadn't even gotten in the car when I started creating a prayer that I could use every morning to get rid of my anxiety. I had a strong desire to get rid of it. It was as if the prayer was sent to me, because it came out without thinking:

Father God, my creator.
Now and today I am free of anxiety.
Help me, Father, so it may be.

I immediately started dealing with the anxiety, saying the prayer every morning. Although I prayed each morning for a long time, I still felt the anxiety and was losing faith that this was the solution. During a session with Guðbjörg, I told her that I was following all her advice, but it didn't seem to help ease the anxiety. I still had anxiety and felt uneasy.

She looked at me for a long time. "I know why it doesn't work," she finally said.

I looked at her in surprise and asked, "Well, what is it?"

She smiled and replied, "You need to place your mind inside your heart and speak to your Father and creator from your emotions. You need to do so sincerely and humbly. We pray from the heart and not from the head. The connection with God is through the heart and the feelings. When you pray from the heart, your prayer is heard. The Savior said that we should come to God like little innocent children."

I accepted and understood everything Guðbjörg said. After a moment of silence, she added, "I need to open up your heart and emotions. There is some obstacle that prevents you from being able to channel your feelings. The channeling comes from there and not your head. Practice putting your mind into your chest and continue saying this prayer. Then you will get rid of your anxiety. That's a promise. When you are about to cry, and ideally you really need to cry, then you are praying with your emotions. You need to beg God for help."

Spiritual Awakening

I looked at Guðbjörg for a long time, taking in all that she had told me and taught me. "What are you thinking?" Guðbjörg asked as she stared at me.

"I am accepting what you were teaching me. It's a lot to take in. I hear that I have a lot left unlearned in my journey."

She smiled. "You must learn until the soul leaves the body," she replied. "I am still learning and have been doing this for many, many years. But it's just fun."

I continued saying the prayer every morning, but now with more depth and with my feelings. I put more and more sincerity into it, and I felt how the prayer became deeper and more sincere every day.

> Father God, my creator.
> Now and today I am free of anxiety.
> Help me, Father, so it may be.

After saying the prayer every morning for almost four months and being aware of my thoughts and pushing away those of them that I knew would cause me anxiety, it finally happened. All of a sudden, when I was driving to work and had just finished praying, it was as if a large stone had been removed from my abdomen. I experienced great relief. It was like I had no stomach at all. Then I realized that I had carried this stone, this weight of anxiety, in my stomach for many years. My chest filled with gratitude and joy, and I started thanking God, my creator, for his help. This was a major milestone on my journey to well-being.

One weekend after I had been completely free from anxiety for many months, a lot of anxiety suddenly washed over me, and I felt a lot of discomfort and pain in my stomach. I had never experienced so much anxiety before. It was a big disappointment, as life had become so wonderful. It was a very difficult weekend, and I couldn't get anything done or even leave the house. I was sick with anxiety.

I contacted Guðbjörg and got my fixed time moved from Thursday to Monday. "I have to see you as soon as possible," I said into the phone.

"I am always ready to help you, my dear friend," she replied.

By Monday morning I was feeling better; the anxiety seemed to be easing. I went to Guðbjörg's in the afternoon and described the fit of anxiety I had experienced. She looked at me for a long time before saying, "I recognize this. The anxiety was visiting you for the last time, and it does so forcefully. This will pass and won't happen again. It happened to me as well. I had one fit of anxiety long after the anxiety was gone, and it was precisely very difficult like you describe. But then it was over."

I was very relieved to hear this. "I thought I had relapsed," I admitted, "and the anxiety was here to stay."

Guðbjörg quickly answered, "It's not like that. You have nothing to fear, dear friend."

Spiritual Awakening

I was relieved when I said goodbye to Guðbjörg and thanked her with a warm hug. From this moment on, I finally said goodbye to the anxiety that had followed me since childhood. "Life is wonderful," I thought to myself as I walked to the car.

While I was driving to work after my session with Guðbjörg, I started thinking, "This spiritual opening and awakening is like walking along a narrow road. The road can be smooth at times, but very bumpy and difficult to pass at other points. There are many obstacles in one's way, but also pleasant experiences. On my back I have a backpack full of stones of different sizes. My task is to pick one stone at a time from the bag to make it lighter, and the journey gets easier with each stone I remove. Anxiety was one of the bigger rocks I had in my bag. Another heavy stone was forgiveness." This manifestation came so clearly to me. I saw my journey vividly.

During my appointment with Guðbjörg a week later, I told her about how I saw my journey in a simple and easy-to-understand way, seeing it picking heavy stones from my backpack and the journey becoming easier.

Guðbjörg smiled and said, "Those are your spiritual guides. You have started receiving messages and information from them without knowing. They explain things in simple ways and with parables. It will just keep going. All of a sudden, you know a bunch of things you had no idea about. That's them. You are connected. Even if you can't channel them properly, this is a start. This is great progress. You are on the right track."

Ragnar Viktor Karlsson

Although my connection with my spiritual guides was increasing, my prayers began to change. I began to pray more to God and Jesus Christ. I felt that my prayers became deeper and more sincere every day. It reminded me of when my mother was teaching me the Lord's Prayer as a small child on Ásvallagata. I began to feel the same calmness and peace when I prayed to God as I did then.

I began to ask God for guidance along my spiritual journey, especially with helping others.

I drove most days from Reykjavík to Akranes to work, leaving early to avoid the morning traffic. I arrived at work at seven o'clock. While I was driving, I began talking to Jesus. I asked him to help me and guide me so that I could help others. I often thought of when he came and stood next to me in the office in Reykjavík. The love and energy I experienced was both indescribable and unforgettable. One day when I was driving to work in the morning dark, I started talking to Jesus, and I asked him to be with me so that I could experience his love again. A few minutes later, a great love began to swell in my heart, and I sensed that he was with me in the car. This great love filled my heart, and tears started to run down my cheeks. Finally, the tears burst forth. I did not see Jesus, but I knew and felt his energy and presence. As I approached Akranes, this wonderful energy and love left me. I stopped crying and said aloud, "Thank you for coming to me, my dear friend." This happened a few times while I drove to work in the morning, and each time I cried.

Spiritual Awakening

I asked Guðbjörg why I always started crying when I felt this love and energy in my heart. "This love is so great, and in the beginning we react like this. It's normal. You'll get used to the energy, and then you'll stop crying and will enjoy the love and be able to share it with others."

I looked at Guðbjörg for a long time. Finally, I said, "I was wondering how I can channel the energy if I'm always crying."

Guðbjörg smiled. "You'll carry this energy and be able to convey it to the people," she assured me. I took in everything Guðbjörg said. After a long silence, she asked, "What are you thinking?"

I looked at her. "I was just thinking about what a great adventure this spiritual journey is. There's always something new happening. Every day I experience something new. It's indescribable—it's both very challenging and exciting at the same time. This is something I would not have wanted to miss. I have learned so much, and myself and my life have changed so much. I feel as if I have been freed from chains and reborn."

Guðbjörg looked at me happily while I spoke to her and then said, "You are going to experience much more, my dear friend. This is only the beginning." My heart filled with anticipation upon hearing this.

The session with Guðbjörg was ending when I asked, "What is my connection to Jesus? He has been with me so much in this journey. He has both appeared to me and I have seen him in my dreams. Is he what you have called my spiritual guides?"

Guðbjörg gazed at me for a long while, and I was excited to hear what her answer would be. "Viktor," she said, and then there was silence. Finally, she continued, "You are so curious. All of this will be revealed in time. Stay true to him and keep talking to him. Ask him to help you, guide you, and comfort you. You will get the answers later."

I was very curious and desired to know more. Then I told Guðbjörg, "My mother often told me when I was little, 'You will understand when you are older.' I always answered her, 'When will I be older?'"

She smiled and replied, "Exactly. It still applies." She paused before continuing. "I do want to tell you one thing. Be careful never to boast about what you do in the future. We are the people's equals. Please be careful of this, friend."

I looked at her for a long time. "I'll be careful," I replied. "I promise."

Guðbjörg pushed me to get in touch with the woman who channeled Yogananda. I finally did and asked her if she wanted to practice channeling and healing with me. She did, and we decided to meet weekly at her house. I sensed that I was a total beginner at this and that my channeling was not deep. I could feel how the mind sometimes came in and interfered. I told her about this, and she said, "Practice makes perfect. That's why we are here practicing the craft." She channeled Yogananda to me flawlessly. I always received good messages from him, and I learned a lot and was encouraged. Channeling seemed to be easy for her, and she did it flawlessly every time. She told me that a few years ago she lived in New York and was a student at a branch of Yogananda's school and learned there what he taught. In short, it was to find and reconnect with God.

Once, she asked me if I wanted to receive healing from her. She had a healing bench in the room and everything was ready. It sounded exciting, so I accepted it with great gratitude. We entered the room, and the first thing I noticed were pictures of Yogananda all over the walls and on tables and shelves. "This is the master," I said while looking at the pictures.

"Yes, this is my spiritual guide," she said, smiling.

I immediately felt a wonderful energy enter the room, and a great calmness and peace came over me. "I think the healing has already begun," I observed. "I feel so calm and relaxed."

She smiled. "Yes, it's enough to enter the room."

I lay down on the healing bench and got comfortable. She put a blanket over me and asked if I was OK. I said yes. A great calm had come over me, and I experienced a great stillness. She sat down in a chair that was at the end of the bench and said, "Now just relax, my friend, and close your eyes." I felt myself almost falling asleep in a great calm when suddenly I began to sense Yogananda standing at the end of the bench by my head. I felt him place a hand on my forehead. As soon as he touched me, I sensed that there were three Yoganandas standing over me, one at my head and one on either side of me. It was a strong sensation, and I felt great love in my heart. Suddenly, I felt like I was lying on my back in a small oblong rowboat, and it was as if the boat was moving down a narrow river. I saw the sky above me, with wisps of white clouds and tree branches passing by. Then I felt myself fade into unconsciousness. I didn't know what had happened, and I woke up when I heard her say, "Well, friend, let's come back now."

I started to move a little, wondering what had happened. I sat up and looked at her as she sat smiling in the chair. "That was an amazing experience," I said, and I began to describe to her how I had sensed three Yoganandas who were all healing me. I also told her about where I lay in the boat. It was all as real as talking to her was. Then I drifted into unconsciousness and really didn't know what happened. I told her I didn't remember anything, that I had been knocked out.

"How are you feeling now?" she asked, looking at me.

"I feel wonderful, like I've slept for a week. I'm completely rested but very dazed." I stood up and folded the blanket that had been lying on top of me. "I don't know if I'm up to channeling to you after this experience," I said as we walked out of the room.

"It's OK. Should we just call it a day?" she asked. I agreed and thanked her. We said goodbye after this unforgettable adventure.

A few days later, I had a session with Guðbjörg. I described what had happened during the meditation. Guðbjörg listened attentively. "This must have been a fun experience," she said. Then she asked, "How did you manage to channel to her?"

I was a bit ashamed and said, "I couldn't do it. I was so dazed from the healing that I couldn't channel."

Guðbjörg looked at me and said, "We always have to give back when we are training two and two together. We must both receive and give. Remember this in the future."

I was aware of this and was ashamed of my performance. "I know this. I have to make it up to her the next time we meet," I replied softly.

"Other than that, how are you doing?" Guðbjörg asked me, and the conversation lightened up.

"I was going to mention to you that sometimes I feel tension and a pain in my chest. Sometimes it feels like my chest is popping out."

Guðbjörg listened attentively. "The heart center is being opened, friend," she said. "Sometimes it happens violently. It will pass. As I have told you, I need to open up your emotional field and heart better. Make you cry and release old sorrows. I perceive sadness in your heart. It will be your homework to find the sadness and cry it out."

I listened carefully, thinking about what she said for a long time. Then I asked, "How do I find the sadness? What should I do?"

Guðbjörg replied, "You should get comfortable in a chair or lie down now. Or you can go for a walk if you think that's better. Then go over your life to find if there was an incident in the past where you experienced great sadness. There might be multiple instances. You should put your mind into this sadness and then cry it out. Often, it is old sorrows that lie in our chest and prevent the energy of love from entering our hearts. The goal is to fill our hearts with love and then pass it on to others. When you have cleared away the grief, you need to remember in the future when you feel grief to immediately go through the grieving process and release the grief by crying when you need to cry. Don't hold back the tears, because then you're just locking up the grief and postponing the settlement. The grief is inside us until we've gone through the grieving process."

I sat and listened to every word that Guðbjörg said. "That sounds like a simple homework assignment," I thought to myself.

When I left Guðbjörg, I started thinking about how I should do this, and when I got home from work later that day, I decided to go for a long walk. I started going through my life year by year, going back as far as I could remember. There was no incident that moved me or touched my feelings. So I returned home from my walk and rested before sitting down in a chair and closing my eyes. Then I did the same as before. I went through my life year after year. The result was the same. Nothing moved me. I did this every day after work for a week, but nothing seemed to work. I returned to Guðbjörg and told her that I hadn't finished my homework. I described to her what I had done.

"You did everything right," she said. "Keep going like that and eventually it will work out," she assured me.

I accepted this and replied, "I will do that."

Guðbjörg smiled. "You are a conscientious and diligent student."

I felt proud at the praise from my teacher.

My desire to help others and to make a difference was so strong that I was willing to do whatever it took to make that happen. After a long silence, I said to Guðbjörg, "In my prayer, I pray that I will always be able to teach people the truth. We live in a world of illusions, and people need to know the truth about life, existence, others, and, last but not least, the truth about themselves."

She smiled. "Exactly."

When I got home, I continued with my homework to release the sadness. I once again went for a long walk through the Elliðaárdalur Valley. After a long time and many attempts, I finally found an incident from my past when I had experienced great sadness and trauma. This was when I was twelve years old, and my mother and stepfather divorced. It was a big shock to me, and I felt a lot of sadness in my heart at that time. "This is the sadness

I'm looking for. I've finally found it," I thought to myself. But now I had to cry out the sadness to ease my heart.

I decided to go home and make myself comfortable in a chair and try to cry my sadness out. I thought more and more about this time and tried as hard as I could to cry. But nothing happened. After a long time, I decided to stop and try again later. It went like this for a few days—I couldn't cry my sadness out. "My emotional field is closed, as Guðbjörg has told me many times," I thought. After several days and many attempts, I finally remembered the music that strongly reminded me of this time period. I found it, and through listening to it, I was able to put my mind more and more into the past. At last, what I had been waiting for happened, and tears began to flow down my cheeks. I cried for a long time. I felt how good it was to cry and how it eased my heart. It was like a heavy slab had been lifted off my chest. "What a relief," I thought as the sobs began to subside. "Another stone gone from the backpack."

It was Saturday and the weather was clear and bright. The sun cast a yellowish light into our living room in Krummahólar. "It's a beautiful day," I thought to myself as I looked out the living room window. My wife Halldóra had gone out to run some errands, so I was alone in the house. I suddenly felt a great and wonderful energy come over me. "I'm going to enjoy this energy," I thought. I sat down on the couch and closed my eyes. I felt more and more energy entering my body, and I started getting goosebumps all over. I had been sitting there for a while when I suddenly saw Jesus standing in front of me. He was wearing a beautiful white tunic, with a full beard and hair down to his shoulders. He held his arms out and said, "My dear friend, this is my love." I sat there in silence. As soon as Jesus had spoken, I began to feel as if water was running down my head, down my throat, and into my chest. Finally, the flow reached my heart, and I experienced the greatest love I had ever experienced in my life. Tears ran like streams down my cheeks, and I saw Jesus slowly disappearing from my sight. Again, I cried for a long time.

Just as before, I didn't fully realize until many days later what had happened. I was wide awake, and it was as real as looking at another living person on the living room floor. It was a profound and unforgettable experience that touched me very deeply.

During the spring of 2018, the phone rang from a Norwegian number. It was the Norwegian company that had let me go a year and a half earlier. They asked where I was and if I could help them for three weeks. At that time, I had a lot of vacation days and wanted to travel again, so I agreed without thinking too much about it. I knew Halldóra really wanted to go to Norway again. I told the Icelandic engineering office that I intended to use part of my summer vacation for this project, and two days later I was back in Norway. It was nice to see my old colleagues again. I had always liked that job, as a lot of good people worked there. I hadn't been there long when I realized my time there was going to be longer than the three weeks we had agreed upon. I therefore made an agreement to do the work from Iceland, but I would come to Norway when necessary.

It was spring and warm in Norway when I arrived there after a long absence. I stayed at a hotel in town and liked it there. On my first night, I decided to go for a walk, taking the same route I had used to take to work a few years before. There I had experienced my spiritual awakening, seeing visions of how a few individuals controlled and ruled the world and through their actions managed to cause many people great distress, suffering, and even death.

"This is where it all started," I thought as I walked along the footpath. "This is much longer than I remembered," I thought to myself with a smile. It felt good to be back there, and I enjoyed walking around, smelling the trees and listening to the birds that had come to begin their springtime work. It was good to walk around and meditate there.

Even though Halldóra joined me once in a while on the work trips, I was often alone, and sometimes I stayed for two to three weeks at a time in Norway and worked from Iceland via the computer in between. I informed the company in Iceland that this would take a long time and asked for a year's unpaid leave. They accepted, and I continued to work in Norway and was more or less there during the whole summer of 2018. I felt that this was what I needed for my spiritual journey. Since I was alone a lot, I used my free time for meditation, either in an armchair in the hotel room or on my walks. I went for long walks every day after work, and the summer in Norway was warm and pleasant. I continued to see Guðbjörg, still doing my best to visit her weekly when I was in Iceland. Sometimes I didn't see her for a while if I stayed longer than a week in Norway.

I was in Iceland when Guðbjörg called and told me that Thoth wanted to see me. So I made an appointment with her the next day. Meeting Thoth was always exciting and very interesting. Something great always happened at the meetings with him.

I drove to Guðbjörg the next day as agreed. "Welcome," Guðbjörg said with a smile when, as always, I sat down on the couch across from her. She stood up, pushed the coffee table away, and said, "Today we need the space because Thoth is going to operate on you." I listened to Guðbjörg attentively. "You're so grounded that it stops you from raising your frequency and reaching higher. You are grounded here," Guðbjörg said, pointing to her neck. Then she added, "Thoth is going to put a plug in your stomach chakra so that the grounding doesn't reach further than your stomach. Then you will be able to connect the upper chakras and reach a higher frequency and consciousness. Are you up for it? We won't do anything unless you give permission."

I listened carefully to what Guðbjörg said and then answered, "I accept all the help I can get so that I can help others."

"You are brave, my friend," Guðbjörg stated, and then she began connecting to Thoth. After a short while, she stood up. In a deep and determined voice, she said, "Stand up, my friend."

Thoth walked closer to me. He pointed his hand to my stomach and began to move it back and forth. I felt the energy start moving within me as I stood with my eyes closed. After a short time, Thoth said, "It's over now, my friend. Just look at the changes that will befall you now." He sat down and Guðbjörg returned.

"That was remarkable," she said, "but now you will make great progress, my friend."

I smiled. "That's good to hear," I replied.

Guðbjörg seemed a bit dazed, but she continued, "Your ego is also still in the way. You need to let the soul, your true self, emerge and rule your life. Be yourself." I listened, taking in everything she said. She added, "You are an eternal soul in a mortal body. Do you understand this?"

I thought so and answered yes.

Guðbjörg peered at me for a long time. "We need the ego to be able to live here on Earth in the body. It is part of our defense system. The task is to let the ego stop controlling our lives and let the soul take over," she explained.

Again, I listened carefully to everything she said. "I understand," I answered.

A few days after this session, I started to feel much more energy in my body. I was in Norway on a business trip, and at the end of the workday I lay down for about half an hour in the hotel room and then decided to go for a long walk. I began to meditate on what Guðbjörg had said about me being an eternal soul in a mortal body. After pondering this for a long time, I suddenly found myself accepting this statement. And, when I did so, I felt a heavy weight lifted from me. "I am an eternal soul," I said aloud as I walked along the path. Despite having heard and read this many times before, this was the first time I understood and accepted it. The body, I now recognized, is the vehicle of the soul during its stay here on Earth to develop and grow. In the end, it leaves the body as empty of worldly things as when it arrived. I own nothing here on Earth; everything is borrowed. I don't even own my body—it is borrowed from Mother Earth and returned to her at the end of life. Nothing can destroy an eternal soul. From that moment on, I have feared neither life nor death.

"It's strange to accept this only now after having heard it countless times before," I thought to myself. It was such a powerful experience, and I felt a great lightness and great freedom.

All anxiety, fear, and worry were now gone from my life. I was finally enjoying every moment. I stopped thinking about the wrongs of the past and about the future. For the first time in years, I was enjoying the moment. I was beginning to live life to the fullest. I saw now that I had always had my mind on either the past or the future and that I had been missing life due to looking out the window of the moment.

Ragnar Viktor Karlsson

"Life is a wonderful gift from God," I told myself as I walked along the trails in Norway. There I smelled the trees and vegetation and listened to the birds singing all around me. I listened to the whispering of the leaves on the trees and the singing of the birds. "This is God talking to me." I took a deep, determined breath in through my nose and then slowly exhaled through my mouth. I felt a lot of energy in my body and a lot of love in my heart.

Father God, my creator.
I thank you for your guidance and blessing.

When I was alone for days and weeks in Norway, I started to pray more and more to God, and I sensed how my prayers became deeper and more sincere every day. I had started experiencing ecstasy and loving energy when I meditated. At the end of the workday, I hurried to the hotel and sat down in the armchair on the hotel balcony, where I closed my eyes and inhaled the energy through my nose and then slowly exhaled. I immediately felt an abundance of energy and love flow through my heart and body. I could sit there for hours with my heart full of love. Now I understood why spiritual gurus could sit motionless in meditation for hours on end in complete stillness. "There is a big difference between the meditations now and when I was starting out," I realized as I got up from the chair after a long meditation. "Then I felt no energy in my body, and ten minutes felt like an eternity." I usually went for long walks after meditating. I perceived that this great solitude in Norway, where I was alone with myself, helped me make

Spiritual Awakening

a lot of progress. I could feel the energy I was taking in growing deeper and deeper each day.

One night when I was lying in bed looking up at the ceiling in the hotel room, I began to pray to God:

Almighty Father—God, my creator.
I thank you for your protection, blessing, and guidance today.
I thank you, Father, for being safe and sound.
I thank you for having a room and a bed to sleep in and for you feeding and clothing me.
These are your gifts, and for them I thank you from the bottom of my heart.

I suddenly said the prayer aloud without thinking at all. It unfolded from me as if reading from a page. I felt that my heart was filled with love while I prayed to God. Prayer now became a bigger and bigger part of my life, and I spoke to God directly from my heart.

It was Saturday, and I got up and drew aside the curtains to see the sun shining outside the hotel window. "A lovely day," I thought to myself. After the morning chores, I sat down in the armchair and prayed to God:

Almighty Father—God, my creator.
I thank you for this day that has come.
I thank you that I am safe and sound
and for being allowed to sleep and rest.
I ask for your blessing, protection, and guidance today.

Ragnar Viktor Karlsson

I had now begun to thank God from the bottom of my heart for my health, shelter, food, and clothing, things I had taken for granted until now. I felt in my heart that these were all gifts from God and that nothing was to be taken for granted in this world.

After the prayer, I went for a long walk and enjoyed strolling along and looking at nature. I went down to a small beach nearby. When I got there, I sat down on a bench and looked out at the calm sea. The only sound I heard was birdsong. "Life is a wonderful gift from God," I thought. "There was no yesterday and there is no tomorrow, only this moment." I had finally learned to live life and enjoy it to the fullest, both during work and play. After sitting there for quite some time, I decided to go back to the hotel. There I sat down in the armchair and began to meditate. I cleared my mind and drew the energy down into my chest. I sensed that a great and wonderful energy had entered my body, and I began to pray:

Almighty Father—God, my creator.
I thank you for this wonderful time at the beach.
I thank you for enjoying and experiencing . . .

I felt my heart fill with more love, and ever more energy came to me. I felt my prayer deepen and come more and more from my emotions and my heart.

I pray for the strength, ability, and courage to help others.
Help me, Father, to help others.
May I show others the way I have walked;

may I help people go from fear and darkness to love and light.

My heart was filled with more and more love with each word, and I felt the tears start to run down my cheeks as I burst out crying from the love, and I called out through the sobs:

Help me, Father—God, my creator, I am your child. Let me enter the Kingdom of God and experience your love and energy.

I had just spoken when I felt my energy and consciousness flow out of my body and into the room. I had become a part of everything that was around me. I had never experienced so much love in my heart. I was experiencing pure ecstasy. As I sat in the armchair, everything joined together. I didn't know how long it lasted, but after a good while it was as if I came back, and I opened my eyes. I felt like I had slept for a long time. I sat there for a while before I felt I could get up from the chair. "This was God I connected with. This was the Kingdom of God," I realized as I stood up. I was very dazed, so I went to bed and slept for a long time.

When I woke up, I thought to myself, "I have found the Kingdom of God, the highest goal of every human being. I have walked the path to life. Now my goal is to teach as many people as possible to follow this very path."

The Teachings of Jesus Christ

When I arrived in Iceland, I went to Guðbjörg and described to her what I had experienced. She listened to me attentively, and then she said, "That's lovely, my dear friend. You have come home."

We then talked about many things during the session, but finally I said to her, "Denmark is starting to strongly enter my mind. Am I being directed there? Should I work there in the future? Maybe we should buy an old manor house and start a spiritual school there."

Guðbjörg again listened carefully to what I said. "That's interesting. Let the thoughts flow and see what happens," Guðbjörg said with a smile.

"But what about teaching and helping Icelanders?" I asked after thinking for a while.

Guðbjörg answered quickly, "You can teach in both places. You could come here and rent a hall for the weekend and hold a course or lecture. It shouldn't stop you."

I got goosebumps when we talked about me teaching and helping others.

"Now our session is over," Guðbjörg said, looking at her watch.

"Every session is like a single moment," I answered and got up.

Guðbjörg followed close behind as I walked to the lobby. "I'm proud of you, my friend. You are a diligent student. Keep talking to God and continue to pray diligently. There is no other way," Guðbjörg concluded, and we said goodbye with a hug.

Soon after that I was back in Norway for work. All my free time was now spent on prayer, meditation, and walks. The prayers became shorter and simpler by the day.

Bless me, Father—God, my creator.

I also talked a lot with Jesus Christ during the walks and in my prayers. I began to think more and more about him and his teaching. He came more frequently into my mind. On the internet, I found a film about his life as it appears in the Bible. I felt how the movie affected me because I felt great love and great energy when I watched it and listened to the words of Jesus Christ. There were also short video clips from the film where one lesson or topic was covered. At first as I watched, I felt tears rolling down my cheeks from the love I felt in my heart, but later I started to carry the energy and the tears stopped.

For the first time in my life, I understood everything that Jesus had said and taught. All the parables and his teaching were now very familiar to me, and they resonated with me deeply. This was what I needed for my journey. I saw that his teachings were just as relevant to people today as they were two thousand years ago. Out of all the spiritual teachings I had seen and heard online, I fully understood only his. I also remembered the times when he came to me vividly to help me along. When I watched the video where Jesus gives sight to the blind man, I strongly felt that he was opening his eyes to the truth about life and existence, especially the truth about himself and his true purpose in life, which was to reach a connection with God.

I was now able to receive messages from above, and sometimes when I was meditating in a chair or on a walk, it was as if I was attending a lecture, and I effortlessly received everything that came to me. It was as if this was all a comfortable and easy refresher. All this now happened unconsciously, and I recalled what Guðbjörg had said to me long before: "When you forget yourself, the information comes down to you."

One time, I had barely started on my walk when information began to flow to me. "You are an eternal soul in a mortal body. The soul lives many lives here on Earth and gets to experience all that earthly life has to offer. The ultimate goal of every human being is ultimately to connect with God in their heart and thereby end their earthly lives and gain eternal life in heaven. The soul is the divine within you and the disposition of the soul is:

Truth
Love
Unity.

"The ego is also within you, as it allows the soul to stay in the body here on Earth. Without the ego you could not live. It is part of your defense system. With the ego, you experience yourself as a limited individual in the body. The ego keeps you from God and prevents the connection with God in the heart. For a long time, it is the ego that controls your life and actions, but gradually, as the soul ages, the ego's influence on life diminishes and the soul, the divine within you, takes control.

"The disposition of the ego is the opposite of the soul:

Deception
Fear
Division.

"Then there is the personality that creates your characteristics as a person and is different from life to life. Being shy, reserved, frank, assertive, or forgiving is a reflection of the personality or the mind. That is where the thoughts are. You control your thoughts, actions, and words here on Earth. When your thoughts are negative and evil, the ego is nourished, and the soul is similarly malnourished. When the ego thrives, it dominates your behavior and decisions. The ego then sends thoughts into the mind that often create great anxiety and fear, which then in turn feeds the ego. It's a cycle that continues until you take action and start replacing negative thoughts with positive ones and evil thoughts with loving ones. Then you begin to feed the soul and feed the ego.

"If this is done for long enough, the soul will finally take control of life, your eyes will open to the truth, and your fear will gradually decrease. Eventually, you will become fearless and free of anxiety. Love comes to you gradually, and you become loving toward yourself and others. He who achieves this saves his soul and finds the Kingdom of God within himself. The world order and those who rule the world rule from the ego, and deception is used to create great fear and to divide people. What Jesus taught people led to the liberation of the soul from the ego, and therefore he was called the Messiah.

"The ego is called Satan in the Bible. It creates temptations that lead people away from the Kingdom of God. The person who is controlled by ego lives in the lower realm, but the person who is on the soul side of life lives in the Kingdom of God. The lower realm and the Kingdom of God are levels of consciousness and are what you experience in your life. God gave man free will, and it is up to each person where he wants to live and be. Therefore, it is important to be aware of your thoughts, actions, and words. Being positive and loving toward yourself and others leads to a higher consciousness and is the path to the Kingdom of God."

Suddenly, I heard birds singing again as I walked along the footpath. I had forgotten time and place while I was receiving this information. "That was a lecture I have received," I thought to myself.

A few days later, it was time to return to Iceland. The work trip was over, and I took the train to the airport in Oslo. I now enjoyed being around a lot of people, like at airports and on the train, where all kinds of people were gathered. I started observing the passersby. It was the first time that my heart began to rejoice to see families, couples with one or two children, at the airport on their way to a vacation, where everyone was happy. "There is nothing more beautiful than a happy family," I thought as I sat at the airport waiting for my flight. This was a common sight during the summertime, as everyone was going south on vacation.

I had started working remotely in Iceland for the company in Norway, and I continued to go for walks and to the hot tub at the swimming pool in the neighborhood after work. I felt there was less energy inside me when I was at home in Iceland than when I was in Norway. There was more tension in the environment in Iceland. But I enjoyed walking around Elliðaárdalur Valley and listening to the birds sing and smelling the scent of the birch trees in the forest. "This is wonderful," I thought to myself every time I walked around there.

One morning, I started working as usual, but soon I began to experience an overwhelming sadness that only grew and grew. Finally, the sadness became so great that I burst into tears and cried for a long time. Then it subsided a bit but came back and ended with me crying a lot once again. I had cried for almost the entire morning, and I didn't even know why. I called Guðbjörg and asked for a session as soon as possible because I didn't know what was going on. "Come at one o'clock today, my dear friend. Let's take a look at this together," Guðbjörg reassured me.

I went to her and sat down on the couch, my eyes swollen and aching from crying, and described what I had experienced and gone through that morning. After a long silence she finally said, "This is the ego letting go of you and the soul taking control of your life. You have conquered the ego and the false self. Your true self has emerged."

I listened attentively, as this was what I had been informed about on my walk during my most recent trip to Norway. "Does the ego die?" I asked after another silence.

Guðbjörg smiled. "No, we can't live without it in the body. It steps aside and stops controlling our lives. But it can intervene every now and then. So we always need to be aware when it happens and stop it before we go off track."

I smiled as well and said, "I'm so grateful to have found you as a teacher and mentor. You can follow me all the way and guide me in everything that comes up along the way."

She nodded her gratitude. "Thank you for the kind words, my dear friend. It's been my pleasure. You have sometimes been a demanding student, and the progress has sometimes been slow. But you have been conscientious and have never given up, and that is why it has worked out."

I was thoughtful for a while. I was still recovering after the sadness and crying earlier in the morning.

"What are you thinking of, my friend?" Guðbjörg asked.

"Nothing special. I'm almost empty inside now," I answered. Then I added, "In the schools, I gained knowledge, but with you I have gained wisdom, the wisdom of life."

229

Guðbjörg looked at me with a smile. She said, "Thank you, my dear friend."

I added, "With wisdom, the consciousness rises and the soul matures. These are the eternal valuables and treasures."

Guðbjörg peered at me. "A lot has changed since I first saw you."

I agreed. "Absolutely. When I first came here to get information and knowledge, I was full of anxiety, fear, worry, and stress. My mind was either in the past or the future, and life passed me by. Now I am free from all this and live in love and enjoy every moment of life. Soon I'll be ready to make a difference and teach others what I have learned here with you."

The session was over, and I said goodbye to Guðbjörg. I thanked her deeply for helping me and allowing me to come at such short notice. "You totally saved me," I finally said.

That night I lay down on my pillow and spread the blanket over me.

Almighty Father—God, my creator.
I thank you for this day that has now passed.
Thank you for your blessing, protection, and guidance.
I thank you for being safe and sound.
I thank you for the shelter, food, and clothing.
Thy will be done, Father.

Spiritual Awakening

I drifted into the dream world, and I dreamed that I was standing next to Jesus Christ and that before us was a grassy field. Rarely had I seen a green color so bright and beautiful. Beyond the field stood a church, and not far from it stood the parish hall. I looked at Jesus, who said nothing. No one else was visible. Finally, the door of the church opened and a group of priests walked out. They were all dressed in their black vestments, their large white collars prominent. All of them came out of the church and walked in single file along a light gravel path toward the parish hall. They disappeared one by one into the house. Then Jesus said, "Come, friend. Let us watch."

We walked along the field to the church and entered. All the priests were standing there in the middle of the floor. There was a lot of noise. I noticed that none of the priests paid any attention to us as we entered. We went to the back of the hall and took up position there. From there, we watched what was going on. After a good while, a middle-aged priestess entered the house, and the noise gradually subsided. All the priests turned to her and watched as she walked up to the stage that was right there next to the exit. She raised her hand and said, "Dear friends, I have apologized for what happened. Now I ask for your forgiveness and your permission to resume my work as a parish priest here." When she had spoken, a great uproar arose and shouts began to be heard. "Be gone! We don't want you in our ranks." I saw that the woman was very down, and she wiped tears from her cheeks. Someone called from the hall, "Be gone!"

I glanced at Jesus. I pitied the woman, and I could feel it moved my heart. At last, the woman walked out, and the door closed behind her. Jesus and I went out and walked to the same place where we had stood initially. There we saw the field, the church, and the parish hall. After a while, the door of the parish hall opened and the priests came out. They walked in single file back toward the church. When everyone had gone into the church and everything had become quiet, Jesus turned to me, looked into my eyes, and said, "My dear friend, how many of them do you think have experienced my love in their hearts and understood and accepted my word and my teachings?"

Then I woke up and immediately sensed that it was one of those dreams with a strong message. It had a strong influence on me. When I woke up, I thanked Jesus for this information and experience.

I thought a lot about this dream. "Understanding and accepting what is said is the way to gain wisdom," I told myself. A few days later, I arrived at the hotel in Norway. I continued to watch videos about Jesus and his teachings. I watched the story about the lost sheep and immediately understood that the lambs that are so often around Jesus in pictures represent the souls that he is saving and showing the way to life, into the Kingdom of God. "The farmer had a hundred sheep and one of them was lost, but the other ninety-nine were in pasture. He went looking for the lost sheep, and after a few days he found the sheep and brought it back to the village on his shoulders. There was great joy among relatives and friends. In the same way, there is great joy in the kingdom of heaven when the sinful soul repents and walks the way to God."

Then came the story about the woman who was to be stoned for adultery and Jesus was asked what he would do. He answered, "He among you who is without sin cast the first stone." Through this account, I understood not to judge others, because he who judges will be judged. I prayed to God after watching this video:

Almighty Father—God, my creator.
I am not one to cast the first stone.
I repent of my wrongdoings and ask for forgiveness for my sins.

Then I watched the story about the house built on sand. "Whoever hears my words and obeys them can be compared to a man who builds his house on rock. A storm hits and the house withstands it. In the same way, whoever hears my words and does not follow them is like a foolish man who builds his house on sand. A storm hits and the house falls. Its fall will be great." He who cultivates himself and frees his soul from darkness and fear and walks the path to life accumulates spiritual wealth for eternity on a strong foundation. He who accumulates worldly values and wealth around egoistic thinking disappears from life with nothing. For all that is earthly will eventually pass away and be left behind.

I felt great changes in myself when I interacted with others. Before, I had been shy and reserved and said nothing in work meetings unless absolutely necessary. But now I had started to participate in the meetings and express my opinions. I was outspoken and without shame.

A few days later, I was back in Iceland, and before long I was again sitting on Guðbjörg's couch. I began telling her about Jesus's teaching and how I understood it better than before. "It moves my heart when I watch these videos," I said.

"That's good to hear," Guðbjörg replied. After a long silence, she said, "There is one thing we have yet to clear out of you."

I looked at her in surprise. "Well, what is it?" I asked.

"You need to release old anger that's in your heart."

I didn't expect this. "I thought the purge was over," I replied.

She smiled. "No, it isn't. So I'm going to give you homework. You should go out into nature where you are by yourself and scream as loud as you can for as long as it takes. Then you should go home and rest well because you will be very tired afterward. Then, when you wake up or have rested, you will feel a great relief within you. It will be like a great slab being lifted from your chest." She looked at me for a long time while I took in what she said. "Will you do this?" she finally asked.

"I will," I replied. "This is the assignment," I added. I did not expect this, but I thought, "I'll do what needs to be done."

Spiritual Awakening

I decided to go up to Kistufell where I had walked so many times before. There was no one there, and the fields there were a suitable place for the assignment. I parked my car next to the empty house and walked out into the field. Just as I was about to start screaming, I peered around to see if I was really alone. There was no one to be seen, so now I was going to start. Then a doubt came over me, and I looked around again. It felt like someone was nearby. When I was sure I was alone, I was again about to start, but there was no sound. I could not scream. I was surprised at how difficult it was. After many attempts, I gave up and drove home. "That was weird," I thought. This assignment sounded so simple, so easy, but it really wasn't.

The next day I drove back up to Kistufell, and everything went like the day before. I wasn't sure I was alone there, and I couldn't make a sound. I drove home a second time without any results. Then, on the third day, I drove up to Kistufell and walked even farther than before up to the mountain. After several attempts, I finally managed to scream. I screamed as loud as I could. I screamed for what seemed an eternity and felt how this lightened my heart. Just as Guðbjörg predicated, after screaming, I was tired and dazed, so I was happy and thankful when I managed to make it back to my car. I went straight home and lay down as Guðbjörg had advised me. I slept for a long time, and when I woke up, I felt the lightness inside me. It truly was like a huge slab had been lifted off my chest, and I felt good.

Ragnar Viktor Karlsson

I told Guðbjörg how it had gone and that this homework assignment was much more difficult than I had thought it would be. She listened to my story and said, "You did well. Now space opens up for higher energy."

Halldóra and I turned our minds more and more toward Denmark. We started looking at houses that were for sale and would be suitable for our spiritual center and school. We quickly saw that it would be best to buy a normal residential property at the beginning, and after about two years would be a good time to find a property that would suit our work. So we started to look around and see where we would want to start out. We continued to ponder these things.

Guðbjörg decided to create a group with four of her students. We were supposed to meet at her place every Friday and stay with her for three hours at a time. Those were rewarding sessions, and I learned a lot. We meditated, healed, and then channeled to each other. The sessions were held at Guðbjörg's place for many weeks, but eventually the suggestion was made to move them to our place, where we continued to meet once a week. I had my regular appointment with Guðbjörg once a week as before. A person from the group held the session when I was in Norway on a work trip.

Guðbjörg once suggested that we all go and work in the spiritual center that we were going to establish. My fellow students didn't support the idea, so nothing came of it. This had no effect on our plans, though. Halldóra and I were still determined to establish a spiritual center to help others.

The next time I went to Norway, I continued to watch Jesus's teaching. I watched as Satan tempted him in the wilderness. I sensed that it was the ego with its temptations and how Jesus defeated the ego within. In a different video, Jesus said, "Narrow is the gate and narrow is the way that leads to life, and few find it. Broad is the road that leads to destruction, and many pass through it."

I started to think about my journey, how shocking and difficult it had been at times. Sometimes I had contemplated turning around and giving up. I thought of all the students I met through Guðbjörg over the years who had done just that. There was something inside me, though, that always encouraged me to keep going, and this motivation became even stronger whenever I was about to give up. This is everyone's journey—walking the path to life is the highest goal of every human being.

Meditation and Prayers

Benevolent Father—God my creator.
I ask for your protection, blessing, and guidance today.
Protect me from all evil,
here on Earth as well as in the spiritual worlds.
Give me strength and courage
for my assignment today.
May your will be done.

I now needed meditation and prayer as much as I needed sleep and nourishment. They had become a normal part of my life. Along the way, I had tried and tested several different methods of meditation. I had tried meditating with music, with guidance, and then in silence. I quickly found that silent meditation, which involved drawing energy into my body and heart, worked best for me. I felt how the energy started to heal my body and how refreshed I was after a short meditation. I also meditated during my walks, and that was when I could best absorb information. Then I forgot myself, and information would flow to me. I lived life one day at a time and enjoyed the moment in everything I did, whether it was play or work.

"It is a privilege to live without anxiety, fear, and worry," I said to Guðbjörg during one of our sessions.

She agreed. "It's a big difference and a privilege." Guðbjörg added, "This will be, among other things, what you'll teach people in the future. You'll teach what you have learned and experienced."

I thought about it and said, "I'll pass on the wisdom I have gained here with you to others. That will be my task."

I recalled one of the videos about Jesus that I had watched a while back in Norway. Then after a short silence, I said, "Jesus told his disciples about the sower who sowed seeds. Some of the seeds fell on rocky and dry ground. They withered and died. Others fell on fertile soil and began to grow and flourish and themselves produced seeds. Some multiplied a hundred times, others seventy times and yet others thirty times. The seeds signify his words and teachings.

"Those who neither understand nor accept his words and teachings can be compared to the rocky and dry soil. The knowledge doesn't pass beyond the person and dies there. Those who understand and accept are represented by the fertile soil because they can begin to teach others what they have heard, understood, and accepted. In this way, one disciple can teach many, and thus, the words and teaching are multiplied and pass from person to person."

Guðbjörg sat and listened attentively. "Quite right. You're starting to achieve a deep understanding," she said.

"Everything is so simple," I answered with a smile. Then I added, "The teachings of Jesus Christ apply so well to this journey that I'm on. They guide me on my way to life."

Spiritual Awakening

After a long silence, Guðbjörg said, "Now I would like to do a meditation session with you. How do you like the idea?"

I answered immediately, "I like it a lot. It's been a while since I have meditated here with you."

As Guðbjörg got up from the chair, she said, "I want to take you on a journey."

I looked at Guðbjörg and asked, "How should we go about this?"

She pushed the table away from the sofa where I sat and said, "You should lie down on the sofa under a blanket. I'm going to sit here on a chair close to your head and lead you during the meditation."

I liked the idea, so I stood up from the couch and got a blanket. I lay down on the couch and pulled the blanket over me. I felt my whole body begin to relax.

Guðbjörg brought a chair from the dining room and sat down next to my head. She put one hand on my chest and said, "Close your eyes and relax, my dear friend. Breathe deeply through your nose, all the way into your stomach, and then breathe slowly out through your mouth."

I did this a few times and felt myself calm down more and more. A great sense of well-being came over me. When I was completely calm and relaxed, Guðbjörg said, "Now, imagine that you are standing on the ground, and suddenly you start flying into the air at great speed." I listened to what Guðbjörg said as I lay on the sofa. She continued, "You are now rotating higher and higher."

I began to perceive that I went through colors: red, orange, yellow, green, and blue. Finally, I entered a purple color. I spent a long time flying through the purple until I entered a white color. Everything was now white, and it was as if I was flying through a cloud. I eventually stopped flying, and it seemed like I had gone as far up as possible. Everything around me was white. A layer of fog lay all over everything, and the fog was moving.

"What do you see?" Guðbjörg asked softly.

I described the fog and what I saw.

"Isn't there a bench over there on the right?" she asked.

I mumbled my answer: "Yes."

She continued to lead the meditation, saying, "Walk over to the bench and take a seat."

I did so and began to look closer at this white mist that surrounded everything.

"Doesn't something happen or appear?" Guðbjörg asked.

I answered softly, "There's a building appearing over there in the fog, a big and beautiful building." I looked at the building standing there in the distance.

"Is there no one there?"

Spiritual Awakening

I started to look closer into the fog, but I didn't see anyone. After a while, I saw someone walk from the building. As the person got closer, I could see more clearly what he looked like. He was a man in a snow-white robe with a golden belt. His hair was completely white, as was the beard that reached down to his chest. His skin was very light and almost white. When he came closer to where I sat on the bench, I saw that he was about two and a half meters tall. I described to Guðbjörg everything I saw and felt.

When the man walked over to me and stood in front of me, he gently said, "Dear friend, finally we meet. Do you want to come with me?"

I thought he seemed familiar, but I could not quite place him.

"We've been waiting for you," he said as we walked toward the building.

I did not answer but walked alongside the man. As we approached the building, I saw how big it was. Several steps led to the front door, which was a large double door. There were columns on either side of it.

"Join me inside, my dear friend," the man said as we walked up the steps.

I was quite excited to see what awaited us beyond the door.

"Welcome," he said as he opened the large door.

Inside there was a huge common room. There stood many men who looked like the man who had come to get me and escort me to the house. The men greeted me by smiling and nodding to me. They came up to me and formed a circle around me, seemingly examining me. There appeared to be more space or rooms on either side of the common room. But the room on the left closest to the entrance had walls and a door made of glass. The walls seemed about five to six meters tall. Everything inside was made of marble. I looked into the room with the glass walls and saw a medical bench in the middle of it. I continued to describe to Guðbjörg what I saw and felt.

"Come with me, my dear friend," said the tall man. He led me into the room with the bench. "You have nothing to fear or worry about, my dear friend," said the man as he gestured for me to lie down on the bench. "We are going to give you our energy."

I lay down on the bench and looked out into the common room. I saw that the men still stood there and seemed to be talking to each other.

"I'm going to stick this in your armpit. That's how we'll pump the energy into you," said the man, who was standing by the bench and holding a tube that seemed to be about the size of a garden hose. The man must have seen the fear in my eyes when I looked at the tube and saw how thick it was. He smiled and said, "Don't be afraid, friend. You won't feel it because here with us, there is no pain." Before I knew it, he said, "Well, my friend, the hose is in its place. Now just lie here and be comfortable. I'll be just outside in the meantime."

I saw him walk out the glass door, go to the other men, and talk to them. I saw that they all turned around and looked at me after he said something to them. I looked around the white room. It was empty except for the bench I was lying on. I couldn't see where the hose came from. It was as if it just lay on the floor, and I couldn't see its other end. Soon I felt that I was falling asleep. I felt my body being filled with a wonderful ecstatic energy and my heart fill with love. I tried to stay awake, but I felt my eyelids getting heavier and heavier. Finally, I couldn't keep my eyes open and passed out. I felt myself fading into unconsciousness. The next thing I sensed was the sound of Guðbjörg's voice through my sleep.

She said, "My dear friend, you can come back when you are ready."

I slowly opened my eyes and saw that I was back in Guðbjörg's living room. It took me a moment to realize where I was, but then I remembered. I looked at Guðbjörg, who sat next to me smiling. It was comfortable to wake up with her there by my side. It took me a long time to wake up, and I lay on the couch for a while. Finally, I sat up, put on my glasses, and saw Guðbjörg, who had moved to her chair.

"This was quite an experience," I said, half-dazed.

"It was wonderful," answered Guðbjörg with a smile.

Ragnar Viktor Karlsson

"Who were they?" I asked curiously.

"They were your spiritual guide. You can always go back there if you want to. Now you know the way."

What Guðbjörg had told me long ago turned out to be true: "Sometimes we don't realize what has happened until the day after." The statement was very fitting here because at first, I didn't understand what had happened. I felt great changes in my body and that the energy and love was much greater than before. Then I realized that this had actually happened. I began to understand and accept that the difference between the physical and the spiritual was not so great after all.

In my next session with Guðbjörg, I told her that I felt a big difference in the energy in my body and that it was much greater than before. Then I told her, "It's remarkable that after all this time and everything you've taught me, I'm still experiencing and learning new things. You still surprise me. I am thankful that I found you and that you became my teacher."

She smiled and thanked me for the kind words. I didn't have the courage to tell her this when we were starting out. Then I didn't dare to say what was on my mind. "That's a big difference and improvement," I thought to myself.

I had sometimes found the teaching disorganized and felt like we moved from one thing to another. I didn't see the context of what she was teaching me and making me do. But when I look back, I see that her teaching was very organized and concise. Everything came at the right time, when I needed it and was ready. I was filled with admiration for her talent when I thought about my journey with my teacher. I often told her, "I pray that I will become a successful spiritual teacher like you." Guðbjörg was my guide and marled my way to life. I would not have wanted to go on this journey without guidance and an established path.

Everything that Guðbjörg told me at the beginning of the trip had come true: "You will experience the deepest sorrows and also a love you have never experienced before, a love that will make you cry. You will walk through dark valleys and go over the highest mountains. I will follow you and show you the way, my dear friend. That is a promise." Guðbjörg always kept her promises. Everything she told me at the beginning of the trip had come true, and I got to experience it. It becomes true only when you have experienced it.

I often thank God for giving me Guðbjörg as a mentor and a friend:

Benevolent Father—God my creator.
I thank you for being able to enjoy the company
and teachings of my mentor
Benevolent Father, bless Guðbjörg.

I sometimes sat on the benches at the top of Elliðaárdalur and looked over the valley, the city, and the channels. Esjan was there in the distance, watching over the city. I could smell the trees, and the birds' song had never

247

Ragnar Viktor Karlsson

been more beautiful or the colors of nature so deep and bright.

Benevolent Father—God my creator.
I thank you, Father, for what I get to experience and enjoy.
Blessed is your creation.
These are your gifts.

Moving to Denmark

It was 2019, and Denmark appeared stronger and stronger to me and Halldóra. We both wanted to move there and set up our spiritual center in the country, but we decided to buy a single-family home first. Our plan was to find suitable housing for our spiritual work within two years. We put our apartment in Krummahólar on sale in the spring, but the reception wasn't good.

We had begun looking for housing in Denmark and started by finding the area where we wanted to live. After thinking about the matter carefully, we decided to stay in the vicinity of Aalborg. We wanted to live in a small town by the sea.

When summer came, I decided, together with my fellow students, to stop meeting at my house. The meetings were moved to another student's house, so I went there once a week. It was a rewarding and fun time, and we helped each other along the way by sharing what we all experienced. I kept up my tempo and continued to see Guðbjörg once a week. Every day, I went for a long walk through the Elliðaárdalur valley. It was wonderful to listen to the birds that sat on their nests and sang.

Around the middle of June 2019, we received an offer for the apartment. We decided to hand it over on July 1. We started packing our things and put them in storage. Then we handed over the apartment a few days earlier than agreed. We moved to a small summer house in Húsafell, where we planned to live until we relocated to Denmark. We had decided to take the ferry from Seyðisfjörður to Hirtshals. At the time, we started looking for housing around Aalborg and found a recently built and beautiful single-family house with an attractive garden in Hals just outside Aalborg. The place fulfilled all our wishes and was by the sea, so we decided to fly to Denmark to view the house. We both liked it and made an offer, which was accepted. We agreed to take possession of the house on September 1, 2019. Afterward, we flew back to Iceland and went to the summer house. We bought tickets for the ferry at the end of August.

There was a lot happening in the last few weeks before the move. We ordered a container for our stuff and tied up loose ends in Iceland. Despite the busy schedule, we had a wonderful time together in Húsafell and went for walks with each other every day. I also went to a hot tub that was by the house. The weeks passed quickly, and before we knew it, the time had arrived to start the journey to Denmark. We decided to drive north and go from there to Seyðisfjörður, leaving on a sunny day. I had mixed feelings about starting this trip. Our first stop was in Blönduós, where we spent one night in a hotel. The next day, we continued to Halldóra's paternal sister who lived in Gvendarstaðir in Kinn. She lived alone there, where all agriculture had long since been abandoned. It was wonderful to stay in beautiful nature with a wonderful woman. We went for walks and rested well after a busy week. After being there for five days, it was time to continue east to Seyðisfjörður. We said goodbye to this lovely woman. The weather was beautiful with sun and warmth, and I enjoyed looking at the Icelandic nature, the mountains, rivers, streams, and green fields that lay under the mountain slopes.

I looked at Halldóra and said, "Nowhere is the grass greener than in Iceland."

Halldóra looked out the car window and said, "I agree with that."

The ferry left early in the morning, so we decided to spend the night at a guest house on Seyðisfjörður, where we arrived late in the day. We settled in and then went for a walk around the beautiful town, admiring the gorgeous old houses. We checked in for our trip with the ferry at the pier the day before departure and got all our travel papers ready. Then there was nothing else to do the next morning but drive down to the pier. We both slept well at the guest house and packed up our things in the morning before driving down to the port. There was a long line of cars at the ferry. Then Halldóra was told that she should walk aboard, but I drove the car onto the ship. We decided to meet at the cabin that had been assigned to us.

Everything went well. I went to the cabin, and a few minutes later, Halldóra arrived. We settled into the cabin, which had a small window, and then went to see the ferry. There were many restaurants and a lot of entertainment onboard. The cruise was scheduled for forty-eight hours.

We went out to the back deck, where we could look over Seyðisfjörður and at the cars driving into the ship one by one.

"It's amazing how a ferry like this can take so many cars," I said to Halldóra, who looked at the seemingly endless line of cars.

It took a long time to get all the cars and people onboard. When it was done, the ferry left and sailed slowly out of Seyðisfjörður. Halldóra and I stood at the back of the ship for a long time and watched the town slowly disappear. I had mixed feelings about leaving Iceland and going on a new adventure in another country.

For the first few hours, the ship rolled slightly. That was enough to make me feel a little sick, and I lost my appetite. I didn't get any sicker, but Halldóra didn't feel anything. The sickness passed, and we started to explore the ship. I went to look at the itinerary and saw that the ferry was supposed to arrive at the Faroe Islands at three in the morning, stop there for an hour, and then continue to Denmark.

That night, I woke up when the engines in the ship fell silent. I got up, looked out the window, and saw the lights in Þórshöfn. I woke up Halldóra and asked if she wanted to see Þórshöfn. We contented ourselves with looking at the town from the cabin window. After about an hour, the ferry continued to Denmark.

We arrived in Hirtshals at noon on a Saturday, a little over a week before we would take possession of our house.

Spiritual Awakening

We had booked a hotel in Aalborg, where we would stay until then. We drove off the ferry and then straight down to a hotel that was in the eastern part of Aalborg, right next to the school grounds where we had lived many years before. We checked into the hotel and decided to drive around the city and reminisce about the old days. It was a strange feeling to be back there after such a long time. The city had changed little, but a few houses had been added here and there.

That evening, we went for a walk around our old neighborhood and near the school grounds where we had spent a wonderful five years. We also walked around the university district, where little had changed. I thought of the friends we made there, most of whom now lived in Iceland. Many memories came to us when we walked there.

We enjoyed the next few days, which we spent like tourists in the city. We also went on drives through the surrounding countryside. Then we took possession of our house on Sunday, September 1, 2019. We met the real estate agent and the woman who was selling the house. She and her husband had built the house together, but when he fell ill and passed away, she decided to sell it. I sensed that it was difficult for the woman to leave the house and that many emotions arose within her. I asked God to bless her and give her strength.

When I was alone with Halldóra, she said with a smile, "Congratulations, and welcome to Denmark."

I smiled and said, "Congratulations."

The container with our belongings arrived a few days later. Just as we were finishing carrying our things into the house, Halldóra's sister called and informed us that my mother-in-law had become very ill, and it was unknown how long she had left to live. She was over ninety and had stayed at the nursing home in Höfði in Akranes for many years. Halldóra and I visited her mother regularly for a long time. I told Halldóra that we had to buy her a ticket to Iceland, and she departed the next day. I had just finished my summer vacation and started working at the Norwegian job, but this time I did so from Denmark. I drove Halldóra to the airport in Aalborg, and she flew to Iceland via Copenhagen.

When I got home, I sat down in an armchair that stood alone in the middle of the living room floor. There I sat amid all the boxes with our stuff. It overwhelmed me, and I was filled with emptiness and loneliness. "What have I gotten myself into?" I asked myself. I missed Halldóra and dearly missed my family that was now so far away. I missed Guðbjörg and the sessions with her and my fellow students. I began thinking about whether or not I should rent out the house where I currently lived and rent a summer house in Húsafell. I thought that would probably be for the best. The loneliness and longing continued for several days. I decided to call Guðbjörg and ask for comfort.

She said to me, "You have become much more sensitive to all emotions and perceive them much more strongly than before. Be positive; everything is as it should be. This will pass, and you and your family will feel at home there."

I calmed down a lot after hearing from Guðbjörg, but then I said, "I hope my journey will continue, even though we are now separated."

After a short silence, Guðbjörg answered, "Your journey will continue. Be diligent in praying, and go for walks. You are always welcome to call me whenever you want."

I quickly replied, "Thank you."

Guðbjörg continued, "It's when you feel that nothing is happening in your spiritual journey that the biggest changes and progress happen, so don't panic. I will come visit you later, and we will spend some time together."

After this good and constructive conversation, I said goodbye to Guðbjörg.

I still felt half empty inside while staying alone in our new house. But after a few days, I started unpacking the boxes and making it a home. Only then did I feel better. I started walking around the area and quickly saw that it was a lovely place with many beautiful trails, several of which were by the sea. It was wonderful to hear the ocean and see the waves coming ashore. There was also a lot of birdlife all around. I started going for regular walks after work.

Halldóra returned a few weeks later, and we started to set up our home. I felt progressively better, and I liked the calm there. It was lovely to have a little garden where we could walk. We started feeding the birds, and it was a joy to watch them eat right by the living room window. Now these little things, which I had not noticed before, gave me pleasure. Halldóra and I started going for longer walks, and we found a footpath that led from Hals to the nearby bathing beach. The route was mostly by the sea and along the coast. This circular walk took about an hour and a half. We often walked this way on weekends and went for long car rides around the surrounding countryside and towns. We would take lunch with us and enjoy being out in nature. I prayed many times and meditated daily, which had now become a part of my life.

One day, Halldóra and I went to Aalborg and walked through the pedestrian streets of the city. I spotted a store with spiritual goods, and we went inside. There were a lot of spiritual books, incense, scented oils, Buddha statues, crystals, angel cards, and other small things. After we had spent a few minutes looking at the items in the store, a strong message came to me: "Do you notice that there is nothing in here that has to do with Jesus and his teachings?" I looked around more closely and realized that it was true. There was nothing connected to Jesus and his teachings. People involved in spirituality, which has been dressed in a special costume, miss out on all the wisdom he taught. I remembered that the spiritual stores in Iceland had similar products, and Jesus Christ was not among them. "His teachings and wisdom are very relevant today and are some of the best spiritual teachings I had found and received in my spiritual journey," I thought to myself as I took a closer look at what was offered in the store.

In December, I went on a work trip to Norway and, as before, used the time efficiently for meditation, prayer, and walks. One night while sitting in a hotel, I started looking for something online to watch. After searching for a long time, I finally found a lengthy documentary on the life of the Buddha. I decided to watch the movie, which was about a young prince, Siddhartha Gautama, who lived about 2,500 years ago and was born on the Indian peninsula where Nepal is today. For the first years of his life, he lived in great luxury in a large palace. His father wanted him to take over the kingdom and later become king. He lacked nothing in the palace and had servants tend to his every want. He had neither seen nor experienced the suffering that life can bring because he had spent his entire life in the palace.

When Siddhartha came of age, he left the palace for the first time, accompanied by his bodyguards and servants, and traveled to the nearby towns. That was when he saw sick people and poverty for the first time. He witnessed hunger, death, and great suffering among the people. He had not known that such things existed, so they had a profound effect on him. He went back to the palace, deep in thought. For a long time, he reflected on what he had seen and experienced. He thought to himself, "There must be a way to end the people's suffering and death. There must be a solution." He pondered this for a while, as he now had a strong calling to help people.

He finally made the decision to leave the palace and venture out into the world to find ways to help people end their suffering. Abandoning his wife and newborn child, he took his horse and rode off from the palace in the middle of the night. Now, for the first time, he was forced to beg for food and be dependent upon others. He found mentors with whom he started working, but he quickly abandoned their teachings and decided to figure things out on his own. He made various attempts to do so, even starving himself to experience physical suffering. Eventually, he realized that the path to success lay somewhere in the middle, just like a string in a sitar needs to be tuned correctly in order to produce a beautiful sound.

He meditated for longer periods of time. He began dealing with the false self and his ego. After seven years of struggle, he finally sat under the Bodhi tree in a day-long meditation and attained enlightenment. After the experience, he called himself Buddha, the Enlightened One. He asked himself, "Now that I have found a way out of suffering, how can I teach others what I have learned and achieved?" He then dedicated his life to sharing his knowledge and experiences with people. Life is suffering, and we are trapped in the eternal cycle of birth, life, and death. To end this cycle, he taught others to attain perfection and Nirvana. Greed, hatred, envy, and deception should be avoided. To help his followers attain Nirvana, he taught them a special way of life that involved being honest, aware of one's thoughts, and much more.

Spiritual Awakening

It was an impressive film, and I sat thinking for a while after it ended. It was all so familiar. First you discover the suffering, and then you receive a strong calling to do good and help others. You desire to walk the spiritual path, face yourself, and free yourself from fear and delusion. Finally, you begin to teach others to follow the same path. I took a lot of this teaching to heart and put it to good use.

In early 2020, when we had settled in the new house, I felt a strong urge to write another book. The only thing I knew when I started writing was the title: *The Truth*. I had no idea what the book should be about. I took a long walk and realized that it would be a small manual with short chapters that people could read one at a time. It would suit those who were not interested in reading thick and large books. The book was supposed to be about what is inside us, what is outside, and how these things are intertwined and interwoven.

Every night after dinner, I would take a long walk and meditate on the next chapter in the book. When I got home, I would start writing and finish one chapter. This was how I had written all the chapters in the book. Then, one day, I did my usual routine of going for a walk and returning home to write but came up blank. I simply could not find the words. Finally, I received a message that the book was finished. I started reading over the text and correcting any issues that I identified. Then I had a proofreader review the text. Once it had been proofread, the manuscript was ready for printing. After thinking for a while about how to release the book, I eventually found a company in Denmark that publishes books to order.

This process took a long time, and the book was ready for publication just before Christmas 2020. I did not market the book because my thought was to sell it to guests who came to our center. Then I translated the book into English and published it with the same company. Not many copies were sold, as I did not perform any marketing.

Guðbjörg and my mother came to visit us in Denmark at the beginning of 2021. Guðbjörg suggested that we hold a lecture together at Jónshús in Copenhagen. She would handle the first part, and I would take care of the second part. I liked the idea, so we booked the venue for a Friday evening and did a good job of advertising the meeting with Icelanders living in Copenhagen and Denmark.

The day before it was scheduled, we drove together to Copenhagen and stayed with Icelanders who ran a small guest house in Amager. The meeting was scheduled from six to eight on the evening of Friday, February 21, 2021. We arrived at Jónshús in time to set up the hall for the lecture. I had ordered several books, which we brought with us to sell. Halldóra was in charge of selling tickets and books at the entrance. When the hall was ready, the people began to trickle in, and many arrived.

Finally, the meeting started, and Guðbjörg began talking to the people. She was lively and walked among the guests to establish a good connection with each one. When it was my turn to give a lecture, I sat on a chair on the stage and started looking at those who had come to listen to us. The hall was completely silent. Then I started speaking: "You are an eternal soul in a mortal body. He who understands and accepts this fears neither life nor death."

I continued for almost an hour until I heard Guðbjörg say, "That's enough. Are there any questions from the audience?"

Then the lecture ended with applause. I didn't realize how much time had passed, and I felt like I had spoken for only ten minutes. I could have continued for much longer, as I felt like I was just getting started. I was incredibly tired on the following days.

"It's hard, my friend, but you'll get used to it, and you'll learn to carry the energy. Eventually, you won't feel it as much," Guðbjörg told me on the day after the lecture.

The next day, my mother flew to Iceland, and I accompanied her to the airport. Guðbjörg stayed behind with us, and the three of us drove home to Hals together.

"The lecture was good. You did well, boy," said Guðbjörg, who sat in the passenger seat on the way home.

"Thank you," I replied. "I felt a strong longing and emptiness when I said goodbye to my mother at the airport."

Guðbjörg looked at me and said, "Your heart is now open, and you have become more sensitive than before. Let the feelings come out; don't hold them down."

261

The journey progressed well. We had crossed the Great Belt Bridge and had arrived at Funen. After being silent for a good while, I said to Guðbjörg, "I've been thinking about something."

Guðbjörg quickly replied, "What is it? Let it out."

I straightened up and said, "When I was looking at this and that spiritual teacher on the internet, I noticed that the teachings were different from teacher to teacher and sometimes completely contradicted each other. Then you could ask yourself, 'Who should I believe?'"

Guðbjörg was quick to answer. "You listen to your feelings and your heart. That's where the truth lies. Now you know the truth and can distinguish it from lies and deception. You will help students in the future to open their eyes to the truth, and then everyone can analyze what they see and experience."

I seconded this. "Absolutely right." After a short silence, I said, "You will know the truth, and the truth will set you free."

Guðbjörg smiled and said, "Exactly."

The trip went well, and we arrived home late in the day. A few days later, Guðbjörg flew to Iceland. To visit her mother, relatives, and friends, Halldóra accompanied Guðbjörg on the flight.

When I was alone at home, I started looking for something on the internet and found an audiobook version of *Tao Te Ching*, which was written by Lao Tzu in 500 BC.

Spiritual Awakening

This was a fascinating read and contained deep and concise wisdom. Every sentence provided unquestionable truth. "Wisdom and truth stand the test of time despite changes in society," I thought to myself after listening to the audiobook and pondering the subject. "The more you listen, the deeper the wisdom."

I walked down to the ocean and watched the sun set.

Blessed is the work of creation, benevolent Father—God my creator.

I said this aloud while I enjoyed looking at the golden and smooth sea in front of me as the sun set.

Halldóra and I started looking for suitable housing for our spiritual center, a dream that had been born about six years ago. We spent a long time searching for housing that suited us and that we could handle financially. Despite several attempts that didn't work out, we finally found a house that seemed like a good fit, so we went to take a look. Located at Falster, it was an old children's school with three large halls, two of which were old classrooms. The third hall was a newer extension. There was also a decent residence connected to the school. We found this to be suitable for what we had in mind. We put up our old house for sale and made an offer on the new house. The purchase was completed at the end of September 2020, and delivery was agreed on March 1, 2021. We started packing and preparing for the move.

We received the house at the end of February 2021. There was a lot of work ahead in painting and getting the rooms ready for lectures and classes. We immediately started fixing the house, which was a lot of work.

In July 2021, my mother and Guðbjörg came to visit, and we paused the construction while they stayed with us. I had a private lesson with Guðbjörg every day. I had left my spiritual path while doing all the work and construction on the house. It was a pleasure to be able to spend so much time with my mentor.

One day, Guðbjörg said to me, "Thoth wants to meet you tonight."

That sounded good. "I like the sound of that," I replied with great anticipation.

After dinner, Guðbjörg asked me, "Are you ready?"

I got up and replied, "I'm ready."

We went into the room where I used to meditate, and we sat down opposite each other. Guðbjörg took off her glasses and said, "I don't know what will happen. But I'm excited to see what he's going to do."

I agreed and started to relax.

"Let's get started," Guðbjörg said, beginning to draw in energy.

Before long, Thoth had come through. It was clear when he arrived, as his energy was so strong and great. Thoth grunted a lot. After a short silence, Thoth stood up and said in a dark and determined voice, "Stand up."

I stood up. Thoth reached out and pointed with all his fingers at my stomach. Then he started moving his hand up and down. I closed my eyes and could feel a great movement of energy in my abdomen. Finally, I felt as if a plug or obstruction had been removed from my stomach. I could feel the energy begin to flow down into my abdomen, as if water was running inside me from my chest.

After a short while, Thoth sat down and said, "That's it, my friend."

Then Thoth left, and Guðbjörg came back. She said, "He did something to your stomach."

I thought about all this and said, "It was like a stream flowing down, like a plug was removed from my stomach."

Guðbjörg stood up and said, "That's it for tonight. Let's go and talk to your mother and Halldóra."

We went into the living room. I thought about it all night, but as I was falling asleep, I remembered the plug that Thoth had put into my stomach a few years earlier to reduce the grounding in my body. "He was pulling the plug out of me," I thought to myself.

The following evening, I had a session with Guðbjörg, and we went back to the room after dinner. I told her that Thoth was removing the plug that he had put into my stomach a few years ago to reduce the grounding.

"That's right," Guðbjörg said, smiling. "Now you don't need it anymore. Now the energy should go all the way to the top of the stomach and base of the spine. Let's look at this together. Close your eyes and relax, my friend." She stood up and began to draw around the energy by waving her hand at my stomach. "Look here," she said softly.

I felt how the energy now went through my head, neck, chest, and—for the first time—down to my stomach. It was great to experience this for the first time. Thus far, the energy had only reached down into my chest to the heart chakra.

"This is wonderful," I said softly.

Guðbjörg sat down. "That's where the energy should be, in the chest," she said. Then she added, "You're making great progress, my friend. Continue to practice drawing the energy in and all the way down to your stomach."

I now felt far more energy in my body. I also experienced great ecstasy when this loving energy finally flowed throughout my body.

"This is the Kingdom of God," I thought to myself. A few days later, it was time for my mother and Guðbjörg to return home. I suggested that Halldóra accompany them to Iceland for a visit. She agreed, and I drove the three of them to the airport. Halldóra planned to stay in Iceland for almost three weeks.

When I returned home, I went straight to meditate and started drawing the energy in and down to my stomach. It was so new and exciting that I had to explore it and experience it better. I had sat down in the chair shortly after noon, and before I knew it, it was ten o'clock in the evening. I had forgotten myself and had been sitting there meditating for about ten hours without realizing it. It felt like only a few minutes had passed. I remembered that when I had started meditating a few years ago, ten minutes seemed like an eternity. "A lot has changed since then," I thought to myself.

The next day, I worked remotely at my Norwegian job. Immediately after work, I had a meal and went straight back to meditating. I meditated until I went to sleep that night. The days passed like this, and then the weekend came. I sat meditating and experiencing this great loving energy in my body from morning to night. During the eighteen days that Halldóra was in Iceland, I used every moment while I was not working to meditate and pray. So, I had been meditating more or less for eighteen days. I felt a big difference in myself, and I sensed much more energy in my body. I had never felt so good before.

When Halldóra came home from Iceland, we continued to build our spiritual center. We wanted to operate legally and in consultation with the municipality, so we applied for a work permit for our activities. We applied for permission to give lectures in the old classrooms. We submitted an application in April 2021. Since we heard nothing from the municipality for several months, I called the office in September of the same year and asked about the status of our application. I was told that it was being processed.

Ragnar Viktor Karlsson

Then more time passed, and we received no feedback or answers. I emailed the municipality in February 2022 to check on the application. I was informed that the application was never received, and we were encouraged to send in a new one, which we did. From February until the summer, we regularly received emails from the municipality indicating that additional data, drawings, and other documents were needed with the application. We spent a lot of time finding these items and sending them to the municipality. The premises were now ready to hold lectures and smaller meetings.

However, the municipality demanded that we have a fire report made for the spaces that we completed and submitted. I contacted the office by phone and asked if we could start operations in the building.

"Operations?" the man on the phone answered in surprise. Then he added, "Now you can start construction and adapt the building to the latest building regulations."

That was when I realized that this mission was over. I knew it would cost a lot of time and money to do what the municipality was asking. We had already spent eighteen months on the application process and were now back to square one. I was angry with myself because I should have known better and what the authorities represented. We had experienced it during the economic collapse in Iceland in 2009, and nothing had changed. "I should have known better," I thought to myself.

It was a big shock for both me and Halldóra. The dream we had for six years was over, and we never even got off the ground. I thought about what we could do. "I want to do good, help people, and teach them all that I have learned and experienced." I still had the strong desire and calling to help people. "I need to do it so that we depend as little as possible on the authorities," I realized.

Finally, I got the idea that it would be best to write books and travel around giving lectures. The old schoolhouse was far too big as a home for the two of us. For my work, I just needed one good room in which to write books. Therefore, we made the decision to sell the house and start looking for a new place to live. We put the house on the market in September 2022. We both wanted to be close to the sea and near an international airport. We considered various places and even thought of moving back to Iceland. However, we soon found that Hals was where we wanted to move. It was there that we would have everything we wanted. There were beautiful hiking trails by the sea, and it was only a short distance to the international airport in Aalborg.

The Graduation

Every year in September, the spiritual fair Light of the World was held in Mosfellsbær over a weekend. The fair would begin with a healing service at the church in Lágafell, which involved a fun mix of mass and healing. Several healers were brought in to heal the attendees. At the fair itself, people would promote products, activities, and treatments. This was a good introduction to all the spiritual work available. Lecturers also appeared throughout the day, with each lecture lasting one hour.

As I felt a strong desire and calling to participate in this event, I volunteered as a healer in the healing service and offered to give one lecture. I was accepted, so I flew to Iceland. I made an appointment with Guðbjörg and asked her if she could prepare me for the healing and the lecture. After making an appointment, I went to see her.

"It's good to be here again," I said with a smile. "Sometimes I miss not being able to come here every week like I used to."

Guðbjörg smiled and said, "It was a wonderful time, but it could be challenging sometimes to make progress with you and to get you through."

I smiled, as I knew what she meant. "It was worth it, as the harvest was millionfold," I said with a smile. "Now I have to start teaching people what I have learned here with you and explain my journey to the people. Because my journey is their journey."

Guðbjörg seconded this.

"I have to write some books, and the first book could cover my journey: *The Way to Life*," I explained.

Guðbjörg listened carefully and said, "Yes, it would need to be published as soon as possible. I just had an idea."

I listened and asked curiously, "Well, what is it?"

"How about I come with you to the lecture and do a little introduction before you start? I would like to introduce you to the people and briefly tell them about you and your journey. How do you like the idea?" Before I could answer, Guðbjörg added, "You can say no; that's fine."

It didn't take me long to make up my mind. I immediately replied, "That's a good idea. I'm up for it."

On the evening of Friday, September 16, 2022, it was time for the healing mass, and Halldóra and I drove to Lágafell Church in Mosfellsbær. Only a few people had come to the church when we arrived, as we were quite early. I went into a room in the back where all the healers met, and we were instructed on how things would go. Although I had not healed much before, I sensed that I was ready for the task. Having received our instructions, the healers and I all entered the church together. When I came forward, stood in front of the altar, and looked over the area, I saw that the church was overflowing with guests and that every seat was occupied. I observed the group as I walked to a seat in the front row. I was very happy to see my mother and her sister there in the church. They sat next to Halldóra in the second row. I was also very happy to see that my uncle had come all the way from the north side of Iceland to see me. His brother was there too. I was very glad to have them join me, and they gave me a lot of support and strength.

The priest started with a short traditional service. When it was over, the healing started. Comfortable calm music was played during the event. Seven chairs had been arranged at the altar for the healing, with two healers working together on each chair. I healed with a woman about my age, and we started receiving people. My hands immediately became very warm. I could feel the energy flowing from my hands to the person in the chair. Each individual received a few minutes of healing, and then room was made for another one. When a young girl sat down in the chair, I immediately noticed that she was wearing black clothes.

"She has sadness in her heart," I thought to myself.

I gently asked her to relax. I sensed a lot of tension in her body, so I put my hands on her shoulders to calm her down. It worked. Then I put one hand on her back and the other on her chest. I was going to let the energy flow through the heart chakra between my hands. But everything was stuck, and I could not generate any flow. It was like a wall existed. I tightened my grip and greatly increased the energy. Finally, I felt the plug come loose, and the energy flowed with great force. When it happened, I felt lightheaded. It was wonderful to experience this. The energy now flowed through the girl's heart center between my hands. She received a lot of energy, and when the healing was over, she stayed put in the chair. She did not want to get up. I put one hand on her shoulder.

"That was wonderful," she said, looking at me.

I smiled at her. "You're welcome. That's why I'm here."

She stood up and hugged me gratefully.

It brought a lot of gratitude to my heart to be able to do good and help people at last. That day in the church, I healed many guests, including both my uncles. However, my last guest was my mother. I did the same to her as I did to the girl and let the energy flow through the heart chakra between my hands. I felt the energy moving, and when my mother stood up, she said, "I could feel how warm your hands were."

I smiled, and my mother walked over to her seat. When all the guests had been healed, the priest concluded the ceremony.

I fell asleep as soon as I lay down on the pillow. It was a great and wonderful experience finally being able to do some good. I woke up refreshed the next morning. It was a big day in my life because I was going to give a lecture at the Heimsljós fair at Lágafellsskóli, a school in Mosfellsbær. I was full of anticipation when Halldóra and

Spiritual Awakening

I began our trip and drove to Guðbjörg. She was getting ready when we arrived, so we had a coffee with her before we continued.

We had brought several copies of my books to sell after the event. Halldóra lined them up in front of the classroom where we were supposed to give the lecture. Guðbjörg and I positioned ourselves at the teacher's table and stood there while the guests settled in the classroom. There were many people present. Eventually, Guðbjörg said to me, "Let's get started." She began to welcome everyone. "Dear friends, today is a big day for Viktor and me because he's graduating as a spiritual teacher and writer."

I looked at Guðbjörg because I didn't know it was graduation day. This was a pleasant surprise to me.

Guðbjörg continued, "Viktor is a miracle. It's a miracle that he has made it through. His calling to do good was and is so strong that he never gave up. Now he is ready to start working."

My heart was filled with gratitude, and a great feeling of victory swept over me. It had been seven years since I began studying under Guðbjörg, and now I was ready to start my work. It was a significant day in my life, September 17, 2022.

Finally, Guðbjörg said with a smile, "Here you go, my friend, the stage is yours."

She took a seat in the front, and I walked out and stood before the blackboard. I looked across the hall and at the people who had come to listen. My mother and her sister were there along with my uncles, as were many other people.

After a long silence, I started speaking. "Dear friends, you are an eternal soul in a mortal body. He who understands and accepts this fears neither life nor death." I then continued to teach and spoke for almost an hour. It passed as a moment. At the end, I thanked everyone profusely for listening.

The people started to get up and leave the hall. Halldóra was at the door and invited people to buy books. We sold all the ones we had brought with us. Halldóra, Guðbjörg, my mother, her sister, and I all went down to the school canteen and had lunch. On the way down to the canteen I said to Guðbjörg, "That was fun."

As she looked at me and patted me on the back, she said, "You did well, boy. You have graduated. Now it's time to start with full force."

When we had eaten lunch, Guðbjörg decided to ride home with my mother and her sister. Halldóra and I planned to take a closer look at the Heimsljós fair and meet the people who were there. We met many people we had not seen for a long time, individuals we had met through our spiritual work. This graduation day was wonderful and memorable.

Spiritual Awakening

A few weeks later, I was walking by our house in Denmark when these parables came to me:

A man lived in a valley surrounded by mountains on three sides. Every morning while he sat drinking his coffee, he looked out the kitchen window at the highest peak in the valley. One morning he thought to himself: "One fine day, I will get to the top and enjoy the view and look over the valley." That's how the mornings passed, and every morning he looked at the peak.

One day, as he stood in the kitchen and looked out the window, he said to himself, "Now I'll climb the mountain and get all the way to the top. I believe I can make it all the way!" He waited for good weather and set off.

It was a long walk to the base of the mountain, but he enjoyed walking through the valley and listening to the birds sing. At last he made it, and he looked up toward the summit. It was much steeper than it appeared from the kitchen, but he thought to himself, "I have faith that I can do this, and I will manage to get to the top."

He began to walk up the mountainside, which was steep and demanding. His steps quickly became heavier. By the time he was halfway to the summit, he was ready to give up. He sat down and looked over the valley. The view had become magnificent. He had never seen the valley from this angle. His house was tiny from up there.

He thought to himself, "I'll give up and head back down." But he was filled with doubt and turned to look toward the summit. "I won't give up now. My faith will carry me the rest of the way," he decided, standing up to continue the journey. With each heavy step, the summit approached. He was tired and now moved very slowly.

Finally, he took the last step. He had made it all the way to the top. He felt a great sense of happiness and victory. He now got to reap the fruits of his labor. He admired the view of the valley and the surrounding countryside. As far as the eye could see in all directions, the land lay beneath his feet. "I did it. Faith carried me all the way, and now I get to experience the view and the blissful feeling of standing here at the top. Faith has turned into experience," he realized as he stood blissfully on top of the mountain.

A certain man was very religious, believing in Jesus Christ and God. He took part in church work, regularly attended mass, and adopted Christian values through love, care, and being helpful.

One day after mass, the man decided to walk through the pleasure garden next to the church. Light gravel paths crisscrossed the grassy garden surrounded by tall trees. Many birds were singing in the treetops in the garden.

He heard a low voice say, "Hello there." He turned around and saw an older man with a short white beard and white hair sitting on a park bench. The man was wearing worn clothes and looked like he was a homeless person who stayed in the park. The old man smiled and lightly tapped the bench next to him with his palm and asked, "May I offer you a seat here in my living room?" The man looked at the old man and did not know whether to continue on his way or sit down with him.

"Actually, I'm on my way home now," said the man, yet walking closer to the old man.

"Now just have a seat, my dear friend," said the old man with a smile.

He walked over to the bench and sat down next to the old man.

"You are coming from the church. Are you a believer?" the old man asked, looking at the man.

"Yes, I am religious and regularly attend mass here."

"What does it mean to be religious?" asked the old man with a smile.

"Well, what can I say?" the man replied, not having a ready answer.

The old man turned to him and said, "It is the highest goal of every human being to experience God's love in its heart and God's energy in its body. It is the way to eternal life. Then you experience the Kingdom of God, which is within you."

The man looked at the old man in surprise. "How can I experience God's love and energy and find the Kingdom of God?"

"You need to face yourself and settle the unresolved issues of your past. Cry out sorrows from the past, and release old anger. Repent for your wrongdoings, and forgive yourself and others. In this way, your heart opens and space is created for God's love and energy. This can be called walking the spiritual path. It is a challenging and difficult journey, and therefore, many turn away before the experience is reached," said the old man. "Follow this, and you will experience it. Put your mind inside your chest, and talk to God from your heart and with your feelings and not your head. Then your prayers will be heard, and God will answer your call."

The man stood up and thanked the old man profusely for his advice. The old man smiled and waved.

The man followed the old man's advice and began to face himself. Weeks and months passed, and the man slowly began to sense changes within him.

One sunny Sunday when he was getting ready to go to church, he thought to himself, "I'm not going to church today, but I'll sit here in the living room and talk directly to God." He sat down and started talking to God with his feelings and heart as he had been advised.

He had been sitting for a long time with his eyes closed when he felt a great energy come into his body. He felt his heart fill with love, and he burst into tears from the great love he experienced.

Spiritual Awakening

"This is God's love and energy that I now experience in my heart and body. This is the Kingdom of God," he realized.

"My faith has turned into an experience.

"I no longer believe in God—I have experienced God."

> Benevolent Father—God my creator.
> Give me strength, ability, and courage
> to do good to others.

Printed in Great Britain
by Amazon